..... gedacht als Abwechslung
zum Wohnungsbau .....

Jan Sparbel
April '94

THE BEST IN
INDUSTRIAL
ARCHITECTURE

THE BEST IN

INDUSTRIAL

ARCHITECTURE

ALAN PHILLIPS

A QUARTO BOOK

Published by ROTOVISION SA
Route Suisse 9
CH-1295 Mies
Switzerland

Copyright © 1992 Quarto Publishing plc
All rights reserved. No part of this publication may
be reproduced, stored in a retrieval system or
transmitted in any form or by any means, electronic,
mechanical, photocopying, recording or otherwise,
without the permission of the copyright holder.

ISBN 2-88046-161-8

This book was designed and produced by
Quarto Publishing plc
6 Blundell Street
London N7 9BH

Creative Director: Richard Dewing
Designer: Chris Dymond
Editor: Viv Croot
Picture Researcher: Jan Croot

Typeset in Great Britain by
Central Southern Typesetters, Eastbourne
Manufactured in Hong Kong by Regent Publishing Services Limited
Printed in Hong Kong by Leefung-Asco Printers Ltd

Contents

Introduction	6
Manufacturing and Engineering Buildings	24
Sheds and Warehouses	68
Laboratories	94
Municipal Architecture	124
Comestibles	168
Transferable Language	192
Natural Factories	216
Index of Projects	222
Directory of Practising Architects	223
Acknowledgements	224

THE BEST IN INDUSTRIAL ARCHITECTURE

Introduction

The closing of the eighteenth century saw the dawn of the Industrial Revolution. The consequent mechanization of society and industry demanded invention and innovation. Just as the religious fervour of the Middle Ages spurred medieval architects to prick the skies of Western Europe with their Gothic spires, pushing structural stonework to its limits, the demand for massive industrial sheds to house mechanized manufacturing processes and the great engines of commerce led architects and engineers to explore and develop the technologies of iron, steel and glass, the only materials that could satisfy their structural requirements.

The Paris Exhibition

Architects Contamin and Dutert designed the Galéries des Machines (Machine Hall) for the 1889 Paris Exhibition using glass and steel. The design owed nothing to history and rapidly established itself as an icon of French 19th century Modernism.

INTRODUCTION

The radicalization of transport systems – particularly the railway – transformed the early 1900s into the age of iron and the engineer, with bridges, railway stations and warehousing establishing the new icons of industrialized society. The early phase of this Factory or Machine Aesthetic was characterized by the use of cast-iron, which had been first used by Abraham Darby in 1777 to build his Iron Bridge at Coalbrookdale, England; it found its apotheosis in the Crystal Palace of Joseph Paxton, built for the Great Exhibition of 1851 in London. The Factory Aesthetic was to change again after the introduction of Henry Bessemer's converter made steel cheap and easily available; steel superseded the limitations of cast- and wrought-iron to establish a new lightness and transparency that declared itself to the world in the buildings made for the Paris Exhibition of 1889.

The Crystal Palace was designed by Joseph Paxton for the Great Exhibition held in Hyde Park, London in 1851. A symbol of the industrial revolution in its innovation, the huge iron and glass structure inspired a generation of buildings which developed their architectural value through engineering systems.

The tireless enthusiasm with which the nineteenth-century engineers and architects embraced the developing technologies was balanced by the influence of contemporary theorists, who counselled caution, claiming the authority of 2,000 years of history and the nobility of the academic tradition.

The Bibliothèque de Ste Geneviève, Paris The vaulted cast-iron framed library by Henri Labrouste established many precedents for future single span steel buildings.

The nineteenth-century French scholar Julien Gaudet (1834–1908) produced the epic theoretical work *Eléments et Théories de L'Architecture*. A pupil of Henri Labrouste (who maintained that history should be understood but not imitated), Gaudet was progressive in establishing an abstract and intellectual view of the importance and relevance of composition in the search for a 'true architecture'.

His contemporary, Auguste Choisy (1841–1909), was more direct. His studies culminated in the *Histoire de L'Architecture*, a reflection on the lessons of architectural history as found in the developing methodologies of construction. Choisy maintained that form would always arise as the logical consequence of technique, and pointed back to the great Gothic cathedrals for an architecture that proved an optimum relationship between form and the fitness of materials to perform their functions.

INTRODUCTION

Choisy's ideas influenced the work of architects such as Auguste Perret (1874–1954) and his pupil Le Corbusier (Charles-Edouard Jeanneret [1887–1965]). This influence was particularly apparent in the legitimization of reinforced concrete as an aesthetically acceptable material; a position that formed an important chapter in the history of modern architecture, although relevant in theory only to the study of industrial buildings as the leading paradigm of tectonic development.

Rue Franklin Apartments at rue Franklin, Paris, built in 1903 by Auguste Perret. Perret's pioneering work with reinforced concrete was influenced by the theories of Choisy and developed by Perret's student, Le Corbusier. The material, developed by civil engineer Joseph Monnier in the 1880s, was cheaper and more versatile than steel; it was closely associated with what became known as the Machine Aesthetic.

Refrigerator Tower, Lyon Tony Garnier's Beaux-Arts Classical education is still evident in the design for the Refrigerator Tower (1913), and yet the influences of the new architecture are such that the building is stripped back to a powerful Minimalist statement that declares the interdependency of Modernism and industrial buildings.

As the technologies developed and the techniques for expressing them became more sophisticated, the scholastic dynasty of Labrouste, Gaudet, Choisy, Perret, Tony Garnier and Le Corbusier gave way to a German enthusiasm for the development of an architecture that sought to harmonize aesthetics and engineering. Influenced by the English Arts and Crafts movement, Hermann Muthesius, an architect and historian originally attached to the German Embassy in London to '. . . appreciate English originality', established a seminal point in the development of a changing relationship between industry and architecture. In 1907 he created the Deutscher Werkbund, a unique organization that sought to continue the mechanization of German production and its subsequent economy with a group of artists, designers and architects. The Werkbund was endorsed by the progressive industrialist, Peter Bruckmann, who prophesied a sharp economic recession if Germany did not overhaul every aspect of its attitude to industry. In the spirit of Gaudet, Bruckmann declared that the image of German products and production could no longer be *'thoughtlessly and shamelessly borrowed from the former treasury of the previous century.'*

INTRODUCTION

The Fagus Factory (1911-1913), where Walter Gropius and Adolf Meyer created an industrial architecture of lightness and transparency. The Fagus building seems an almost direct progenitor of Sant'Elia's call for 'the perfection of technical method, the rational and scientific use of materials'.

The Glass Pavilion The re-emergence of Form and architectonics, found their complete synthesis in Bruno Taut's 1914 Pavilion for the Deutscher Werkbund. The originality of structure, material and technique suggested endless possibilities for the expression of 'New Architecture'.

THE BEST IN INDUSTRIAL ARCHITECTURE

Feeding on this enthusiasm, Muthesius delivered an address to the Werkbund Congress of 1911 entitled 'The Spiritualism of German Production'. To an audience that included Mies Van de Rohe, Walter Gropius, Bruno Taut and Le Corbusier, Muthesius declared:

'Far higher than the material, is the Spiritual, far higher than functions, material and technique, stands Form. These three material aspects might be impeccably handled but – if Form were not – we would still be living in a merely brutish world. So there remains before us an aim, a much higher and more important task – to awaken once more an understanding of Form and the Revival of Architectonic sensibilities.'

The Werkbund and the Bauhaus, set up at Weimar (1919) under the direction of the Belgian architect and ex-patriot Henri Van de Velde (1863–1957), established a design position in response to standardization, mass production and automation that was to be the *tabula rasa* on which would be written the emerging theory of modern architecture, or as Henry-Russell Hitchcock preferred it 'the International Style'.

Werkbund Pavilion, Cologne Sometimes referred to as the Model Factory, the Werkbund Pavilion was completed by Walter Gropius and Adolf Meyer in 1914. It became the physical manifestation of the Werkbund ideologies and the first building of the movement which was to become known as Functionalism.

Centennial Hall, Breslau
Architect Max Berg radicalized the use of reinforced concrete in the Centennial Hall (Jahrhunderthalle) at Breslau (1913). The ability of the material to conquer large spans with relatively slender sections promised it a pivotal role in the history of industrial architecture. However, its maturity, particularly under the hand of Pier Luigi Nervi, was to be found in major public buildings such as the Turin Exhibition Hall (1947) rather than buildings for manufacture and production.

INTRODUCTION

AEG Turbine Hall Peter Behrens was appointed architectural consultant to Allgemeine Elektricitätsgesellschaft (AEG) in the same year, 1907, as Hermann Muthesius founded the Deutscher Werkbund. The two events established an influential relationship between German industry, architecture and design. Behrens AEG Turbine Hall of 1908, however, is still rooted in Classicism compared to the Futurist perspective of Sant'Elia only 16 years later.

When the Bauhaus moved to Dessau in 1925 under the new direction of Walter Gropius (1883–1969) the synthesis between architecture, art, engineering and production was as complete and as influential as any institution has been on the shape of the Factory Aesthetic during the twentieth century.

The Bauhaus, Dessau The creation of a new building by Walter Gropius for the Bauhaus at Dessau could have been designed as a response to Sant'Elia's call for 'a taste for the light and the practical'.

However, it would be impossible to complete this brief sketch of the historical context from which contemporary industrial aesthetic developed without a reference to the Futurist movement.

THE BEST IN INDUSTRIAL ARCHITECTURE

Established under the literary hand of Emilio Fillipo Tommaso Marinetti (1876–1944), it was developed by the powerful and polemical sketches of the young Italian architect Antonio Sant'Elia (1888–1916). In contrast with what Sant'Elia saw as a German fascination for order, monumentalism and a static formalism that was bound to the nineteenth-century tradition of Beaux-Arts composition and planning, the Futurists became obsessed with motion, speed and disorder, the reaction of an old agrarian society waking to the science of trams, electric lights, telephones, sewing machines, and more than all of those, the romance of an emerging and internationally competitive automobile industry.

La Città Nova Sant' Elia's early vision of future cities has become remarkably real during the latter half of the twentieth century.

Lloyds Building, London
The Factory Aesthetic had become institutionalized within an educational framework that was to influence generations of architects, including Sir Richard Rogers, whose Lloyd's Building in London simultaneously reaffirms the Factory Aesthetic as an icon of 1990s Modernism and fulfils Sant'Elia's vision of 'lifts that [must] swarm up the facades like serpents of glass and iron'.

INTRODUCTION

In 1914, Sant'Elia pre-dated the manifestos of the Bauhaus and Le Corbusier by writing a preface – his *Messagio* – to the *Nuove Tendenze Exhibition* which, in its economy of words and powerful polemic, establishes many fundamental tenets of late twentieth-century industrial architectural theory.

It is also extraordinary in being as relevant a manifesto to modern architects working at the closing of the second millenium as it was to Sant'Elia and his European contemporaries at a time when the International Style was still in its infancy. As such, it is proper to quote the whole text of the *Messagio*.

"The problem of Modern architecture is not a problem of rearranging its lines; not a question of finding new mouldings, new architraves for doors and windows; nor of replacing columns, pilasters and corbels with caryatides, hornets and frogs; not a question of leaving a façade bare brick or facing it with stone or plaster; in a word, it has nothing to do with defining formalistic differences between the new buildings and old ones. But to raise the new-built structure on a sane plan, gleaning every benefit of science and technology, setting nobly every demand of our habits and our spirits, rejecting all that is heavy, grotesque and unsympathetic to us (tradition, style, aesthetics, proportion), establishing new forms, new lines, new reasons for existence, solely out of the special conditions of modern living, and its projection as aesthetic value in our sensibilities.

Such an architecture cannot be subject to any law of historical continuity. It must be as new as our state of mind is new, and the contingencies of our moment in history.

The art of building has been able to evolve through time and pass from style to style while maintaining the general character of architecture unchanged, because in history there have been numerous changes of taste brought on by shifts of religious conviction or the successions of political regimes, but few occasioned by profound changes in our conditions of life, changes that discard or overhaul the old conditions, as have the discovery of natural laws, the perfection of technical methods, the rational and scientific use of materials.

In modern life, the process of consequential stylistic development comes to a halt. Architecture, exhausted by tradition, begins again, forcibly, from the beginning.

Calculations of the resistance of materials, the use of reinforced concrete and iron, exclude "Architecture" as understood in the Classical and traditional sense. Modern structural materials and our scientific concepts absolutely do not lend themselves to the disciplines of the historical styles, and are the chief cause of the grotesque aspect of modish constructions where we see the lightness and proud slenderness of girders, the slightness of reinforced concrete bent to the heavy curve of the arch, aping the stolidity of marble.

The formidable antithesis between the modern world and the old is determined by everything that was not there to begin with. Into our lives have entered elements whose very possibility the ancients could not have suspected; material contingencies have crystallized, spiritual attitudes have arisen, with thousand-fold repercussions; first, the formation of a new ideal of beauty, embryonic still and obscure, but already stirring the masses with its fascination. We have lost the sense of the monumental, the massive, the static, and we have enriched our sensibilities with a taste for the light and the practical. We no longer feel ourselves to be the men of the cathedrals and ancient moot halls, but men of the Grand Hotels, railway stations, giant roads, colossal harbours, covered markets, glittering arcades, reconstruction areas and salutary slum clearances.

INTRODUCTION

We must invent and rebuild ex novo *our modern city like an immense and tumultuous shipyard, active, mobile and everywhere dynamic, and the modern building like a gigantic machine.* Lifts must no longer hide away like solitary worms in the stairwells, but the stairs — now useless — must be abolished, and the lifts *must* swarm up the façades like serpents of glass and iron. *The house of cement, iron and glass, without carved or painted ornament, rich only in the inherent beauty of its lines and modelling, extraordinarily brutish in its mechanical simplicity, as big as need dictates, and not merely as zoning rules permit, must rise from the brink of a tumultuous abyss; the street which, itself, will no longer lie like a doormat at the level of the thresholds, but plunge storeys deep into the earth, gathering up the traffic of the metropolis connected for necessary transfers to metal cat-walks and high-speed conveyor belts.*

For these reasons I insist that we must abolish the monumental and the decorative; that we must resolve the problem of Modern architecture without cribbing photographs of China, Persia or Japan, not stultifying ourselves with Vitruvian rules, but with strokes of genius, equipped only with a scientific and technological culture; that everything must be revolutionised; that we must exploit our roofs and put our basements to work; depreciate the importance of façades; transfer questions of taste out of the field of petty mouldings, fiddling capitals and insignificant porticos, into the vaster field of the grouping of masses on the grandest scale; that it is time to have done with funereal commemorative architecture; that architecture must be something more vital than that, and we can best attain that something by blowing sky-high, for a start, all those monuments and monumental pavements, arcades and flights of steps, by digging out our streets and piazzas, by raising the level of the city, by reordering the earth's crust and reducing it to be the servant of our every need and our every fancy.

And I conclude in disfavour of
Modish architecture of every style and nation.
Classically solemn architecture, hieratic, theatrical, decorative, monumental, graceful or pleasing.
Preservation, reconstruction, reproduction of ancient monuments.
Perpendicular and horizontal lines, cubic and pyramidal forms, static, grave, oppressive and absolutely foreign to our newest sensibilities.

Use of materials that are massive, bulky, durable and expensive, all opposed to the complexity of Modern culture and Modern experience.
and I affirm
That the new architecture is the architecture of cold calculation, temerious boldness and simplicity; the architecture of reinforced concrete, iron, glass, textile fibres and all those replacements for wood, stone and brick that make for the attainment in maximum elasticity and lightness.
That real architecture is not, for all that, an arid combination of practicality and utility, but remains art, that is, synthesis and expression.
That decoration, as something superimposed on or attached *to architecture* is an absurdity, *and that only from the use and disposition of raw, naked and violently coloured materials can derive the decorative value of a truly Modern architecture.*

And finally I affirm that just as the ancients draw their inspiration in art from the elements of the natural world, so we — materially and spiritually artificial — must find our inspiration in the new mechanical world we have created, of which architecture must be the fairest expression, the fullest synthesis, the most effective artistic integration."

THE BEST IN INDUSTRIAL ARCHITECTURE

It is a tragic irony that many of the opportunities that would have afforded Sant'Elia's revolutionary re-building of the 'Old City', were created by World War I, in which he died two years after completing this thesis.

The *Messagio* was publically ignored by intellectuals not willing to argue the subtle distancing of Sant'Elia's position from that of the more dangerous and politically active pre-war literati of the Futurist movement. Consequently, the Italian avant-garde gave way to the influence of Le Corbusier, who (in the same year as Theo Van Doesburg synthesized the Dutch Modernist position with the 1923 De Stijl Exhibition at *L'Effort Moderne*) published his *Vers Une Architecture*. This polemical book, coupled with the manifesto of C.I.A.M. (Congrès Internationaux d'Architecture Moderne) continued the tradition of the pre-war Modern movement to manifest itself with many notable industrial buildings, in particular the Van Nelle Factory in Rotterdam (1927–30) by Brinkman, Van der Vlugt and Stam and the Boots Pharmaceutical Factory by the engineer Sir Owen Williams at Beeston, England.

The Boots factory might not have appeared at all if it wasn't for another irony. The Nazi antipathy to internationalism forced the Bauhaus to close in 1933. Its then director, Mies Van de Rohe, moved to the America of Frank Lloyd Wright, while other architects, including Walter Gropius, Eric Mendelsohn and Marcel Breuer came to England to reinforce a nervous respect of the 'New Architecture'. As the Nazi threat became global, so the Modern movement, with its diaspora of architects, became the International Style in fact as well as theory. The great Finnish architect, Alvar Aalto, preached the early Swiss C.I.A.M. gospel in Finland to influence the Scandinavian masters Sven Markelius and Gunnar Asplund, while Russian Berthold Lubetkin left Paris to form the English team of Tecton. In the devastated Europe of 1945, complex theoretical polemics, manifestos, exhibitions and individual buildings of avant-garde virtuosity gave way to the reality of architecture as social service, and of architectural practice led not by

The Boots Factory Reinforced concrete and structural steelwork combine to make a seminal and innovative building, appropriately by the hand of engineer Sir Owen Williams.

the virtuoso but by the brilliant and collective teamwork of national agencies. Public building works, including schools, hospitals, mass housing, town planning and road building, largely triumphed over works of individual genius; the industrial building ceased to be the paradigm of a developing Modernism.

THE BEST IN INDUSTRIAL ARCHITECTURE

But in the United States of America, where World War II had less of a physical effect, the scholastic tradition was continued, and particularly the relationship of theory and practice by the almost unique circumstance of practising architects also holding professorial positions. Together with Mies Van de Rohe (1886–1969), Louis Khan established an extraordinary synthesis between his career as a teacher and his built works, two of the most influential, the Richards Medical Research Laboratories, Philadelphia and the Salk Institute, California, began again within the fields of research and industry. Khan's writings were influential but remain as fragments of ideas rather than a manifesto or theory or holistic ideological position. However, as a link in the chain of the emerging American scholastic dynasty that included Frank Furney, Louis Sullivan and Frank Lloyd Wright, Khan was to become a mentor to the architect and theorist Robert Venturi, who filled the void left by the collapse of Functionalism with his book *Complexity and Contradiction in Architecture*, written in 1962 and sponsored by the Museum of Modern Art (MOMA) that encouraged Hitchcock and Philip Johnson to establish the idea of 'the International Style'.

The Salk Institute Louis Kahn's building continued the tradition of in-situ poured reinforced concrete which was championed by Auguste Perret and developed by Le Corbusier.

The Domino House

Le Corbusier's *esquisse* (preliminary sketch idea); the simple column and two-way reinforced slab construction promoted the far-reaching idea whereby the wall element of any architecture could be understood as a separate entity. Thus the glass curtain wall became available as part of the language of the Factory Aesthetic.

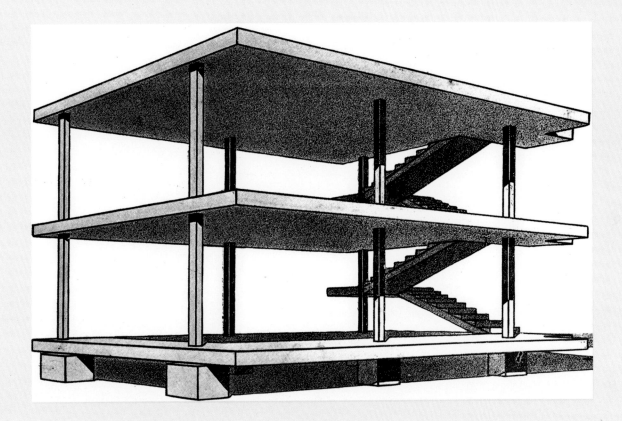

Venturi's thesis, as its title implies, manipulates many of Khan's dictums and quotes many works of Le Corbusier and other modern masters, to claim that great architecture can (and should) be ironically ambiguous, multivalent, disorderly, complex and contradictory — quite the reverse of the Bauhausian and Werkbundian Factory Aesthetic that was referential to the order, simplicity, charity, economy and function of the machine.

As a consequence, and due to the seeming irreconcilability between the polemics of Venturi and the whole functional programs of a typical factory building, industrial architecture was left without a contemporary theoretical manifesto against which to test its conceptualization, and judge its product.

THE BEST IN INDUSTRIAL ARCHITECTURE

Although it is probably not for these reasons that industrial architecture remained largely undistinguished during the 1950s, '60s and '70s, manufacturing companies and service industries seemed satisfied with the ordinariness of a simple, cheap and well-serviced shed, tending to see 'architecture' as a higher art reserved for new universities, public buildings, religion and commerce.

In Britain, the Festival of 1951 declared an end to the postwar austerity and the beginning of a new social and cultural awakening. Architects built theatres, opera houses and museums, while a new phenomenon of anonymous 'design & build' contractors provided shelters for the production of goods that were rarely more than the mere utility of construction.

The commissioning of the British architects Ahrends, Burton and Koralek to build a new diesel engine plant for the American Cummins Engine Company in Scotland established 1975 as the end of this mid-century blight. ABK restored Muthesius' concepts of form to industrial architecture, concentrating on the human condition at work as a basis on which to resolve and synthesize the complex programme requirements of operation and organization. The architecture is intellectual, social, structurally articulate and sometimes quite abstract in its reference and relationship to the local landscape. The building is without metaphor or symbol, and yet expresses its function through a powerful geometry coded behind an anonymous language that skilfully uncouples it from a literal association with the internal combustion engine. The Cummins Factory established a new Industrial Architecture, whose strength lies in the absence of idiomatic device and, ironically, the absence of a ruling manifesto.

INTRODUCTION

Cummins Factory, Scotland The Cummin Diesel Engine plant by English architects Ahrends Burton Koralek signalled the end of 'Industrial Blight'.

The buildings that followed Cummins are all designed upon the collective wisdom of the theories and histories of architecture without the 'thoughtless and shameless borrowing from the former treasury of the previous century', to paraphrase Bruckmann. That has always been the role of Industrial Architecture and the Factory Aesthetic: to celebrate change, encourage innovation and always be new.

Manufacturing and Engineering Buildings

The programme for sheds, warehouses, speculative industrial buildings and, to a lesser degree, laboratories is driven by a requirement for flexibility, economy and standardization and the need for a non-specific or dumb space which can accommodate many variations of many configurations of storage and production processes. In general, the opposite is true in engineering and manufacturing buildings.

Designing a building to accommodate the complex process of manufacturing motor cars, for instance, or a factory to make furniture or engines presents problems of analysis and research that demand very special architectural skills. The kind of analysis required must take in technical, social and theoretical considerations and respond to the complex interrelationship between the hierarchies of management, the needs of the workforce, the requirements of the manufacturing process, equations of efficiency and the ethos of the corporate philosophy. This being done, the architecture will often express an eccentricity in response to the specificity of the problem that carries it beyond the limitations implicit in the shed-duck category system explained in the chapter on *Sheds and Warehouses*.

The Cummins factory at Shotts in Lanarkshire, Scotland by Ahrends, Burton and Koralek defies simple categorization. The architects combine the intuitive, scientific and intellectual to make an architecture that eschews the pedagogy of dogmatic theoretical positions and the self-regarding hedonism of the diva. The strength of ABK's work for Cummins lies in its distance from idiomatic device, stylistic slavery or historical quotation. It is as original and unique as the product it serves and the landscape it respects.

In contrast and comparison, Frank Gehry's chair factory for Vitra in Germany is very duckish. That is not to say that the building is shaped like a giant chair, but its programme, structure and mechanics are submerged by an overall symbolism embodied in the form of a collage of the style system called Deconstruction. Indeed, the architect is so intimidated by the style and its language that a museum or an abattoir or a university would probably look exactly the same, in the same way that a duck-down quilt factory or duck-meat processing plant would always look like a duck and any building whatsoever under the hand of a classical revivalist would be clad in bizarre orchestrations of the antique orders to look like a giant temple.

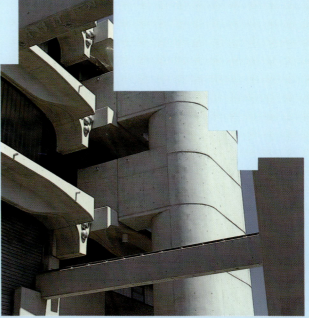

THE BEST IN INDUSTRIAL ARCHITECTURE

Cummins Diesel Factory

'This redevelopment was carried out around and amongst the existing factory buildings, phased to maintain production. The production areas, with a capacity to produce 90 250–400 HP diesel engines a day, have been divided into four distinct elements – Receiving, Machining, Stores and Assembly, Testing and Shipping – placed in a progressive sequence.

Above the east/west production flow there is a separate north/south pedestrian circulation system connecting to the car park at a higher level of the site. The car park stretches the full length of the factory allowing people to park near to their place of work. Three covered bridges provide direct access into the factory at this upper level, clear of materials movement on the floor below. Stairs give access to locker, toilet and refreshment facilities below. The two principal bridges are linked by an upper level amenity deck which contains the Cafeteria, Medical Centre and Lecture Room. Part of the existing factory space has been converted into an open plan office with a high degree of natural light.

The roof structure is designed for the lifting of heavy loads, with the secondary beams forming a level plane below the triangular primary trusses of tubular steelwork. These trusses also form routes for service distribution and incorporate zones of roof glazing.

Energy studies were undertaken. As a result, the buildings are insulated thermally to standards well above the regulation requirements and utilize sophisticated air cleaning and ventilation systems to transfer heat from the high heat producing Machining Areas to adjacent parts of the building. A centralized monitoring system has been installed to control the mechanical, electrical and security systems and to provide maintenance intelligence.

There were also extensive consultations with staff at all levels during the design process in order to obtain detailed and direct knowledge of all aspects of the process as well as creating a sense of investment and participation in the workforce.'

Key

1 Car Park
2 Energy Centre
3 Final Assembly
4 Offices
5 Assembly
6 Canteen Deck
7 Stores
8 Machine Shop
9 Receiving

CASE STUDY

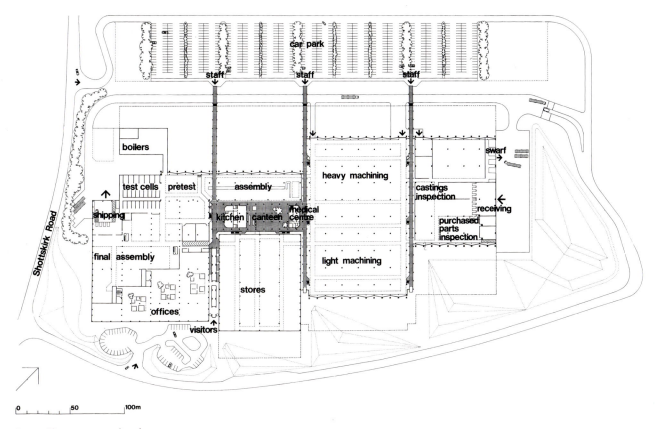

General layout: upper level

Cummins Engine Company Ltd

ARCHITECT: Ahrends Burton Koralek, London, England
CLIENT: Cummins Engine Company Ltd
FUNCTION OF BUILDING: Diesel engine manufacture
LOCATION: Shotts, Lanarkshire, Scotland
SIZE: 50,000m²
DATE OF COMPLETION: 1983
ARCHITECTURAL INTENTION: Ahrends, Burton and Koralek building for Cummins was one of the first to give architecture back to the industrial sector after the collapse of functionalism. Structural articulation and trust in the traditional role of geometry in architecture, together with a humanist approach to the problem solving of a complex programme, establishes the factory as seminal, not only in the history of industrial architecture but in the development of modernism. Set into an artificial landscape that is referential to the tradition of Scottish mining the building sometimes takes on an abstract surreality that confirms its importance.

Cummins Diesel Factory continued over page

THE BEST IN INDUSTRIAL ARCHITECTURE

CASE STUDY

Cummins Diesel Factory continued

29

THE BEST IN INDUSTRIAL ARCHITECTURE

Gateway One

ARCHITECT: Arup Associates, London, England

CLIENT: Wiggins Teape

FUNCTION OF BUILDING: Corporate HQ for paper manufacture

LOCATION: Basingstoke, Hampshire, England

DATE OF COMPLETION: 1980

ARCHITECTURAL INTENTION: The expressed tubular steel structure sits lightly on the ground and rises to articulate the proportions of a large paper manufacturing building.

MANUFACTURING AND ENGINEERING BUILDINGS

Steelcase Industrial Center

ARCHITECT: Greiner Inc, Grand Rapids, Michigan, USA
CLIENT: Steelcase Inc.
FUNCTION OF BUILDING: Computer furniture manufacture
LOCATION: Kentwood, Michigan, USA
SIZE: 850 acres rolling site
DATE OF COMPLETION: Ongoing
ARCHITECTURAL INTENTION: The campus buildings are designed to parallel the craftsmanship and aesthetic appeal of the furniture products manufactured within.

Rounded corners were incorporated into the design to soften their appearance and visually reduce the size of the large structures. Complementary colour tones were used on the panels and serve to identify specific functions within the buildings. In planning the project, a strong emphasis was placed on landscaping, effectively changing the traditional appearance of a manufacturing complex into an attractive and pleasing environment.

Services and people are raised above the ground as if attached to umbilical cords, giving life to the various sections of the Steelcase International manufacturing plant.

David Mellor Cutlery Factory

ARCHITECT: Michael Hopkins and Partners, London, England
CLIENT: David Mellor
FUNCTION OF BUILDING: Cutlery factory
LOCATION: Hathersage, Derbyshire, England
DATE OF COMPLETION: 1988
ARCHITECTURAL INTENTION: The building was commissioned by David Mellor who designs and produces cutlery to sell in his group of kitchenware shops.
The site was a disused gas works in beautiful countryside in an area controlled by the Peak Park Planning Board which insists on designs which respect the Derbyshire vernacular.
An open-plan circular production space was built on the foundations of the old gasometer. A lead roof supported by elegantly detailed radial trusses apparently floats above the solid stone walls.

MANUFACTURING AND ENGINEERING BUILDINGS

THE BEST IN INDUSTRIAL ARCHITECTURE

MANUFACTURING AND ENGINEERING BUILDINGS

The Factory

ARCHITECT: Ben Kelly, London, England
CLIENT: Factory Communications
FUNCTION OF BUILDING: Record production
LOCATION: Manchester, England
SIZE: 850m²
DATE OF COMPLETION: 1989
ARCHITECTURAL INTENTION: Manchester in Northern England is thick with small nineteenth century factory buildings, this one for a long redundant textile business. Many have been lost to the bulldozers of twentieth century expansionism but this one came under the hand of Ben Kelly Design, whose job was top give it new life in the form of a record production facility for the appropriately titled Factory Record Company. The host building is stripped back to reveal the essence of its quality and then reorchestrated by a series of interventions that redefine the new functions and work in surreal juxtaposition to the existing structure. Exposed conduits, stripped back heating systems and carefully articulated light fittings create an interior palimpsest that simultaneously respects and enhances the original building while declaring its own originality and truthfulness to a new function.

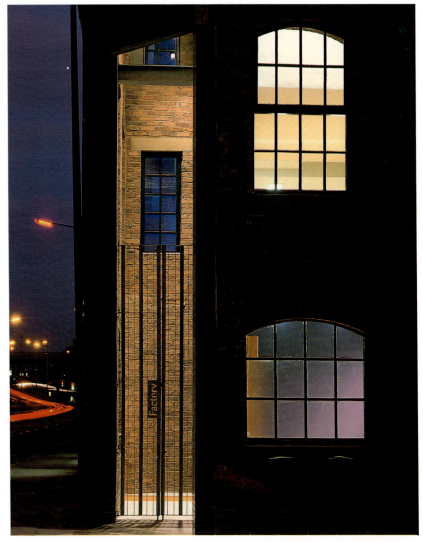

The Factory continued over page

37

The Factory continued

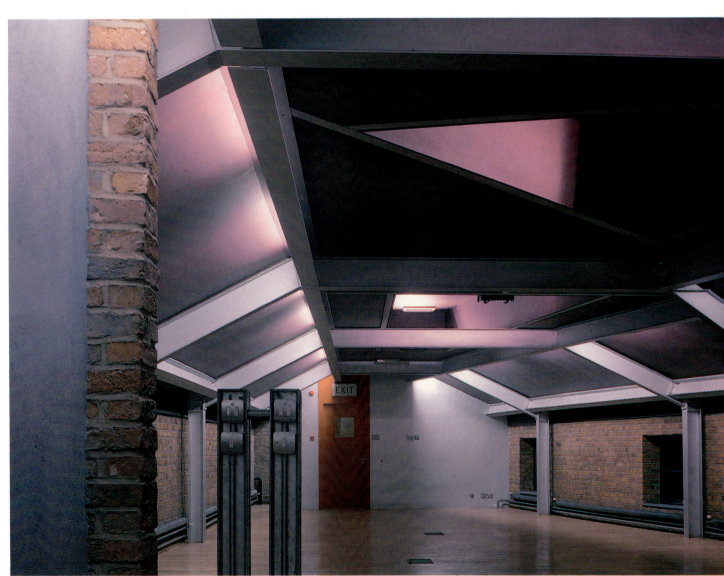

39

THE BEST IN INDUSTRIAL ARCHITECTURE

ORF Radio Station and Studios

ARCHITECT: Professor Gustav Peichl, Vienna, Austria
CLIENT: Österreiches Rundfunk
FUNCTION OF BUILDING: Radio station and studios
LOCATION: Salzburg, Austria
DATE OF COMPLETION: 1972
ARCHITECTURAL INTENTION: The characteristic, unmistakable form of the broadcasting station building is internal function projected outwards. A crucial factor in the design was a request for the possibility of expanding various areas should the need arise. Form thus derives from correct arrangement of interior space and consistent regard for the technical requirements of a broadcasting station.

Both at the front and to the side of the ORF studios at Salzburg, Austrian architect Gustav Peichl has used the complex air conditioning requirements to arrange a number of stainless steel ducts as sculptural landscape markers. In contrast the powerhouse building tries to lose itself at the end of a car parking lot.

MANUFACTURING AND ENGINEERING BUILDINGS

Vitra Chair Manufacturing Facility continued over page

Vitra International Furniture Manufacturing Facility and Design Museum

ARCHITECT: Frank O. Gehry & Associates, Inc, Santa Monica, California, USA

CLIENT: Vitra International, AG

FUNCTION OF BUILDING: Furniture manufacturing facility and design museum

LOCATION: Weil-am-Rhein, Germany

SIZE: Factory: 9,000m^2; museum: 800m^2

DATE OF COMPLETION: November 1989

ARCHITECTURAL INTENTION: The project, situated in a rural landscape bordered by Switzerland and France, had to encompass three major parts: a seating assembly plant with adjacent office, mezzanine and distribution areas; a small furniture museum to house the owner's collection of chairs; and the preparation of a master plan for the site, which includes a new entrance road and gate house, a future expansion of the factory, museum parking and ancillary facilities.

The Vitra building by Frank Gehry has become a contemporary icon of a new architectural movement called deconstructionism. Instead of rhythm, balance, order and scale this new architectural style, which has pretentions to linguistic philosophy, calls for the architecture to be rotated, fractured and formally disaligned.

THE BEST IN INDUSTRIAL ARCHITECTURE

Vitra Chair Manufacturing Facility
continued

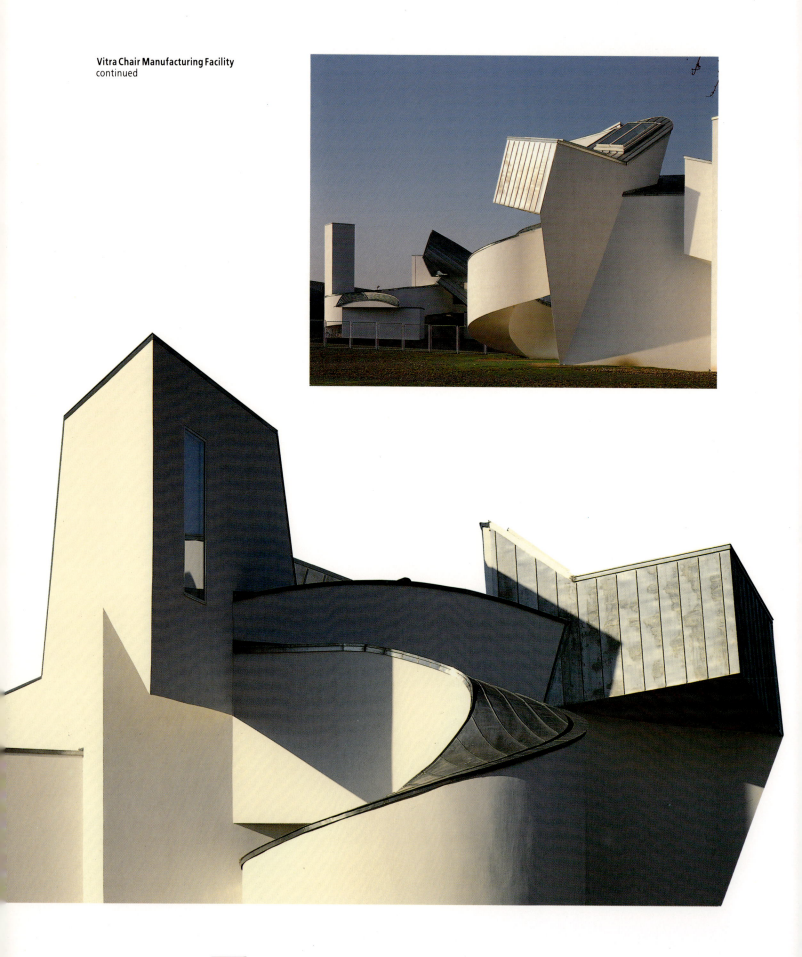

THE BEST IN INDUSTRIAL ARCHITECTURE

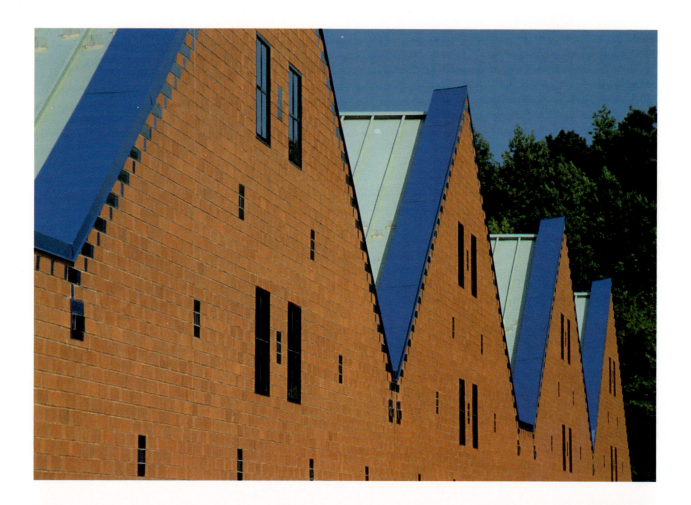

Becton Dickinson Labware Manufacturing Facility

ARCHITECT: Florance Eichbaum Esocoff King Architects, Washington DC, USA

CLIENT: Becton Dickinson & Company

FUNCTION OF BUILDING: Labware manufacturing facility

LOCATION: Durham, North Carolina, USA

SIZE: 188,500sq.ft

DATE OF COMPLETION: April 1991

ARCHITECTURAL INTENTION: A broad, low building is broken into three components to house production, administrative and shipping/storage functions. Roof gables, evocative of local rural architecture, differentiate the three components and diminish the apparent mass. Oversized brick and patterning reduce the scale of otherwise large and blank walls. Polychromy within the brick patterning creates a metaphorical reflection of earth and sky.

Four white steel trusses mark the entrance and indicate the primary structure of the building complex. A row of gables finely detailed in brick and blockwork are sealed with a powerful blue coping as the sawtooth facade meets the sky.

MANUFACTURING AND ENGINEERING BUILDINGS

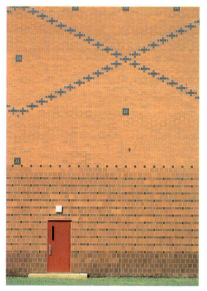

THE BEST IN INDUSTRIAL ARCHITECTURE

Canary Wharf Eastern Access Lifting Bridge and Control Building

ARCHITECT: William Alsop and John Lyall, London, England (Project Architect Peter Clash)

CLIENT: London Docklands Development Council

FUNCTION OF BUILDING: Lifting bridge and control building

LOCATION: Canary Wharf, London, England

DATE OF COMPLETION: 1990

ARCHITECTURAL INTENTION: Although primarily an engineering led project, architects had the remit to provide an overall architectural direction to the development. This involved a design input to the embankment, roadspans, lighting, and landscaping as well as the bridge structures and control building. The design for the bascule bridges is characterised by the decision to make visible the working parts of its counterweight system. The great A-frames, pivots and hydraulic rams supporting the steel bridge spans of 25 metres each are in full view. This was made possible by constructing a separate building adjacent to the bridges for all the hydraulic plant required for the bridges' operation. This in turn provides the support for a control cabin which is dramatically cantilevered up and away from the building allowing maximum visibility of operation.

The small installation at Canary Wharf in London exposes the power of the diagonal and the dynamics of an architecture articulated firmly in the tradition of the functionalist school. The electronic eye perched on the head of the control room is a reminder that the human eye might soon become redundant.

MANUFACTURING AND ENGINEERING BUILDINGS

THE BEST IN INDUSTRIAL ARCHITECTURE

Navy Weapons Workshop

ARCHITECT: Harry Seidler and Associates, Milsons Point, New South Wales, Australia

CLIENT: Australian Navy Defence Department

FUNCTION OF BUILDING: Weapons workshop

LOCATION: Garden Island, Sydney, Australia

SIZE: 33,500m² approximately

DATE OF COMPLETION: 1985

ARCHITECTURAL INTENTION: This is the first stage of a segmental, long building to serve the maintenance needs of warships. The structure is positioned so that a 50-tonne dockside crane can lift heavy components off the ships and deposit these at either end of the building. High-level cranes travel out from the workshop bays and bring the elements inside. The office and amenities wing is placed offset forward so as not to interfere with the continuous line of the high-level crane rails. The structure is of post-tensioned reinforced concrete for the building's frame. Internal flexibility required large spans.

Navy Weapons Workshop continued over page

THE BEST IN INDUSTRIAL ARCHITECTURE

Navy Weapons Workshop continued

MANUFACTURING AND ENGINEERING BUILDINGS

MANUFACTURING AND ENGINEERING BUILDINGS

Advanced Textile Products Factory

ARCHITECT: Nicholas Lacey Jobst & Partners, London, England
CLIENT: Centreland Ltd, for Advanced Textile Products Ltd
FUNCTION OF BUILDING: Headquarters office, storage and manufacturing facility for firm of textile importers
LOCATION: London, England
DATE OF COMPLETION: 1989
ARCHITECTURAL INTENTION: The building was first commissioned in 1984 for the textile importers, Advanced Textile Products Ltd, to provide a speedy, yet imaginative response to their pressing need for new office and warehouse accommodation. Apart from its proximity to the Millwall Dock, it was a design almost without a context. The future of the surrounding land was uncertain and unplanned; awaiting whatever the market might have to offer. The new buildings therefore had to provide their own context, so the offices were designed to make the best possible use of the dock edge and to offer unusually good waterside views from within. Particular attention was also paid to the main entrance. Since this was separated from the street by the larger, blank bulk of the warehouse it called for special emphasis and was thus dramatised by a bold circular motif recalling ATP's trade in rolls of fabric.

The pattern created by glazing and panel joints is dissolved at night when the internal lighting systems dissolve the articulation on the facade to create a transparency that exposes the vertical trunking systems that are expressed as huge yellow columns.

55

THE BEST IN INDUSTRIAL ARCHITECTURE

Financial Times Building

ARCHITECT: Nicholas Grimshaw & Partners, London, England
CLIENT: Financial Times/St Clements Press
FUNCTION OF BUILDING: To house the printing presses and ancillary process accommodation for the Financial Times
LOCATION: East India Dock Road, London, England
DATE OF COMPLETION: Building envelope completed December 1987; fitting out period and installation of presses: January–June 1988
ARCHITECTURAL INTENTION: To create a landmark for the eastern entry to London as the Hoover building is to the western; to display the workings of the printing presses to the outside world through a spectacular 16-metre high and 96-metre long glass wall; to develop specialist glazing and cladding systems approppriate to the building. A pair of silver cylindrical towers mark the entrance to the principal elevation of the Financial Times print works building. The envelope is a contrast between a tight glazed skin, held in place by an ectoskeletal structural rig, and a composition of cladding systems that provide for a grain and texture variation. The building's quality derives not just from the material components, which are largely proprietary, but from their careful arrangement and skillful detailing.

Financial Times Building continued over page

Financial Times Building continued

THE BEST IN INDUSTRIAL ARCHITECTURE

Financial Times Building continued

MANUFACTURING AND ENGINEERING BUILDINGS

Renault Distribution Centre

ARCHITECT: Sir Norman Foster and Partners, London, England

CLIENT: Renault (UK) Limited

FUNCTION OF BUILDING: Parts distribution centre, training schoool, offices and showroom

LOCATION: Swindon, Wiltshire, England

SIZE: 24,000m²

DATE OF COMPLETION: May 1983

ARCHITECTURAL INTENTION: To establish a progressive image of design quality which would extend from the client's product range to their working environments. The site is an irregular sloping plot of 6.5 hectares (approximately 16 acres). The design concept integrates a response to both the site and the brief by using a 'module' which can fill out the site irregularities with the potential for random growth over time. From the outside the building form is articulated by the scale of the individual 'modules', their expressed structures and a coordinating use of the Renault yellow house-colour.

Each building 'module' is 24 metres at the apex and suspended from masts which are 16 metres high. The first stage of construction commprises forty-two 'modules', which accommodate a warehouse, distribution and regional offices with computer installations, a showroom for cars and trucks, an after-sales maintenance engineering training school with associated workshops and seminar rooms, a restaurant and entrance canopy. The initial building ground plan can be expanded by 67%, the suspension structure providing connection points for this to be done without disruptive influences.

The yellow ectoskeletal pylons that help to secure column free production areas also combine as the principal aesthetic to the Renault Factory at Swindon. The declaration and articulation of structural elements as the principal ordering system devices makes Sir Norman Foster's building an icon to an architectural typology that firmly belongs to the evolving tradition and machine style.

Renault Distribution and Parts Centre continued over page

63

Renault Distribution and Parts Centre continued

Sheds and Warehouses

Robert Venturi's 1966 thesis *Complexity and Contradiction* saw one of the first authoritative, scholarly and popular criticism of Functionalism and the Modern movement in architecture. His subsequent book *Learning from Las Vegas* reinforced his position by combining a number of essays to argue that the implicit and predominantly abstract language of the International Style that developed from Modernism and the Machine Aesthetic failed to communicate to a public who were culturally associated with the more literal and explicit iconography of old architecture.

Venturi clarified his argument by introducing the idea of categorizing buildings as either ducks or decorated sheds. According to Venturi, the decorated shed allows the public access to the building's function or meaning by laying on top of the ordinary shed a number of ornamental or decorative devices that endow the structure with a sign or system of signs that declare the building's intention. The term decorated shed therefore describes a building 'where the system of space and structure are directly at the service of the programme with ornament applied directly to them'.

In Victorian England, the rush to mechanization flooded suburbia with cottage industries. Many small factories were knitted into the fabric of a predominantly domestic landscape by siting the production shed at the rear and attaching a front office embellished with a façade or architectural signage that simultaneously symbolized the nature and prestige of the industry within and fulfilled the building's duty to the public realm. Such buildings would be at the centre of Venturi's decorated shed category; a more modern example is John Outram's Kensal Road factory in London.

On the other hand, the duck is a building type in which the systems of space, structure and programme are submerged and distorted by an overall symbolic form. The term is borrowed from Peter Blake's book *God's Own Junkyard* which shows an illustration of a building shaped like a giant duck which houses a shop that sells decoy ducks to Long Islanders. Ducks are central both to the building's function and the building's form: the latter is unequivocal in its explicit iconography and all there for the public to read. Venturi would approve of this, as it seems he would of Phillippe Starck's knife factory in France, which although not knife-shaped has a giant blade thrust through its roof.

To the duck and the decorated shed I should like to propose two additional categories: the composite shed and the silent shed. Many contemporary industrial buildings that have come to be known as high-tech derive their aesthetic from the expression of structure and services. Consequently the systems of space, structure and mechanics are both the servants of the programme and its ornaments or symbol. Buildings of this type, like Sir Richard Rogers' PA Technology Center at Princeton, New Jersey may be described as composite sheds.

Contrary to Venturi's polemic there are still many architects who believe that beauty need only tell its own story, a story which becomes more potent when expressed in simple and abstract terms. Scale, composition and proportion are the building blocks of a language that claims its integrity in the metaphysical world of balance, harmony and poetics; the building's systems support the programme alone in the absence of ornament, symbol and semiotics. This is the silent shed; the warehouse in Igualada, Spain by Correa, Gallardo Mannino Asociados is a beautiful example of this sophisticated category.

Venturi's analysis could be criticised as simplistic, as can the four category analysis offered here; it is not the intention that the four categories should explain all types of current industrial architecture. However, they offer a useful way of ordering a vast catalogue of work and offer an holistic overview of the principal paradigms by which world industrial architecture chooses to express itself.

Centre d'Activités Zac de l'Ourcq

Pantin, to the east of Paris enjoys an industrial heritage. The Ourcq canal, traditionally and historically a route for industrial traffic through the capital runs parallel to modern rapid transport facilities. When the industry along its banks became obsolete, the area fell into decline. For the future of Paris, it is essential that suburbs like Pantin transform themselves, becoming vital parts of the city once more. With the Centre d'Activité, Chemetov and Huidobro are pursuing a preoccupation with urban 'margins' that has influenced their whole career. What could be more natural than to provide workplaces in the town to fill gaps left by disappearing nineteenth century industries? This reasoning led to the building of the multi-functional centre which is in itself a town with grand squares and interior streets with space and facilities for all manner of small enterprises.

Centre d'Activités Zac de l'Ourcq

ARCHITECT: Paul Chemetov and Borja Huidobro, Paris, France
CLIENT: Semiic Promotion
FUNCTION OF BUILDING: Multifunctional workspace, hotel and car park
LOCATION: Pantin, Paris, France
SIZE: 75,668m²
DATE OF COMPLETION: November 1989
ARCHITECTURAL INTENTION: The steel and metal panelled building uses cantilevered canopies, staircase towers and dualistic arrangement of eno and ectoskeletal frames as formal devices in the animation of the speculative industrial building at L'Ours.

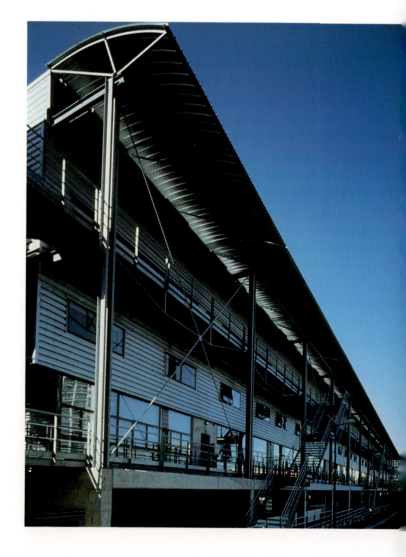

CASE STUDY

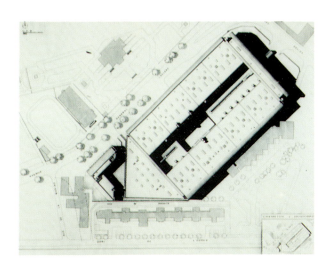

71

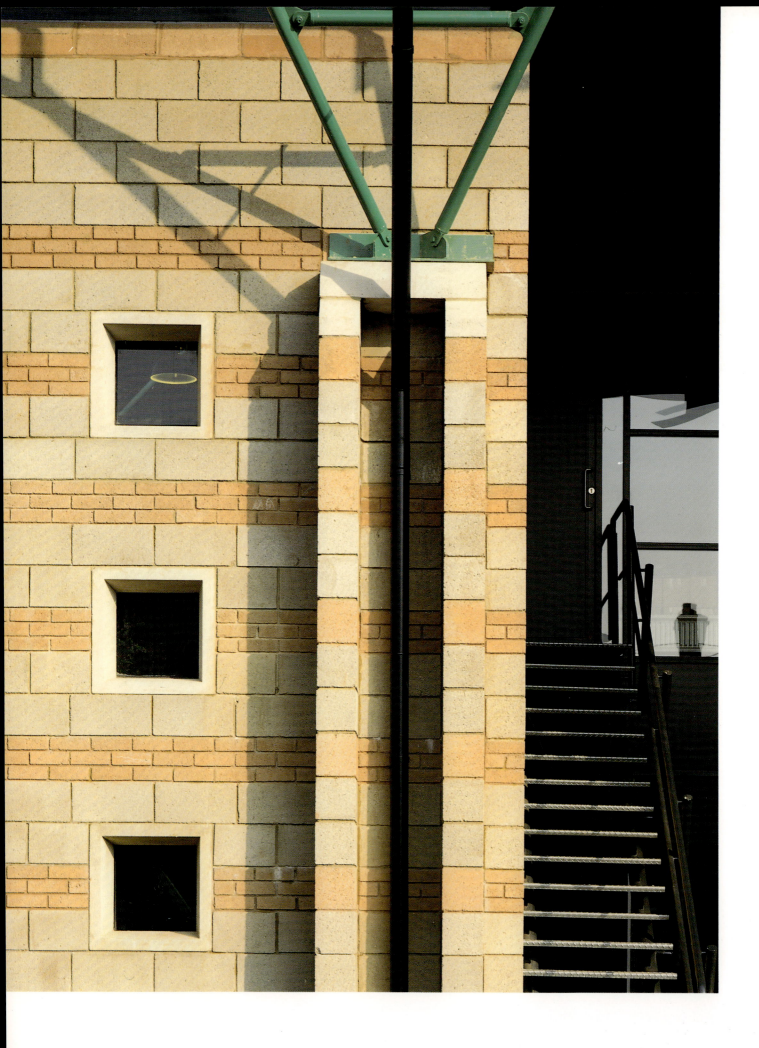

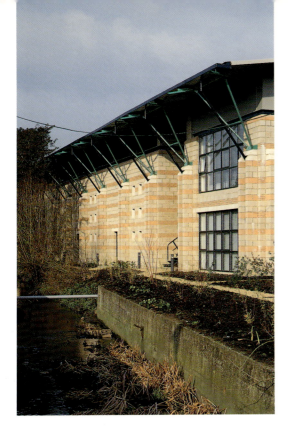

Schwarzkopf Warehouse

ARCHITECT: Denton Scott Associates, Milton Keynes, Buckinghamshire, England

CLIENT: Schwarzkopf Ltd

FUNCTION OF BUILDING: Picking and packing warehouse and offices

LOCATION: Aylesbury, Buckinghamshire, England

SIZE: Warehouse 1800m^2; offices (2 storey) 733m^2

DATE OF COMPLETION: 1988

ARCHITECTURAL INTENTION: To provide an industrial building to upgrade the surrounding rundown area but which was more energy efficient and more architecturally interesting than the conventional "metal clad box". A metal roof with deep protective eaves supported on steel trusses and gutters floats over modular blockwork walls. The substantial walls are subdivided into bays by projecting piers and punctured by groups of openings reflecting the various patterns of usage within the building. The simple grey profile steel shed is piped in yellow to provide a strong silhouette against the sky. Doors, bollards, bumpers and primary supporting structures are also clarified by colour to establish their position as separate architectural elements.

The strong banded masonry base providing an appropriate monumentality gives way to a line of light steel brackets that spring from a twin pier system to support the roof overhead. The building's elegance, simplicity and economy is in marked contrast to its immediate neighbour, by way of confirming that the skill of the architect can always raise the mundane to the sublime.

THE BEST IN INDUSTRIAL ARCHITECTURE

Cargo Warehouse

ARCHITECT: John Outram Partnership, London, England
FUNCTION OF BUILDING: Warehouse
LOCATION: Poyle, London, England
ARCHITECTURAL INTENTION: John Outram's warehousing at Poyle in Surrey is probably unique in the history of sheds and warehousing. The architecture derives from and is referential to an allegorical position wherein a timber framed and glazed skin is stretched across a sequence of simple sheds to form a backdrop or architectonic canvas behind a large "Venetian piazza", over which the trucks and truckers play out a type of mechanised theatre. Inside, the shed ceilings are perforatred with a collection of roof windows that drop puddles of light onto the floor below. As the sun moves across the sky, the light plays against the walls and red structural supports reminiscent of Tiepolo's work to establish another, if obscure, reference to the Venetian allegory. The ordinariness, modesty and economy of the warehouse sheds allows Outram to detail the facades with materials and finishes that are not normally characteristic in the architecture of such a utilitarian building type.

SHEDS AND WAREHOUSES

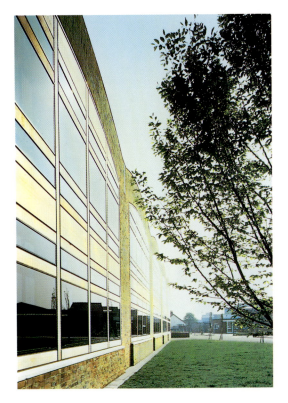

Warehouses at Poyle continued over page

THE BEST IN INDUSTRIAL ARCHITECTURE

Warehouses at Poyle continued

SHEDS AND WAREHOUSES

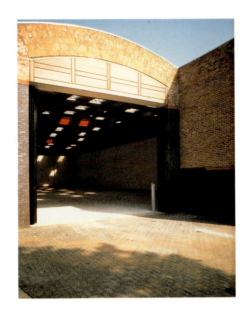

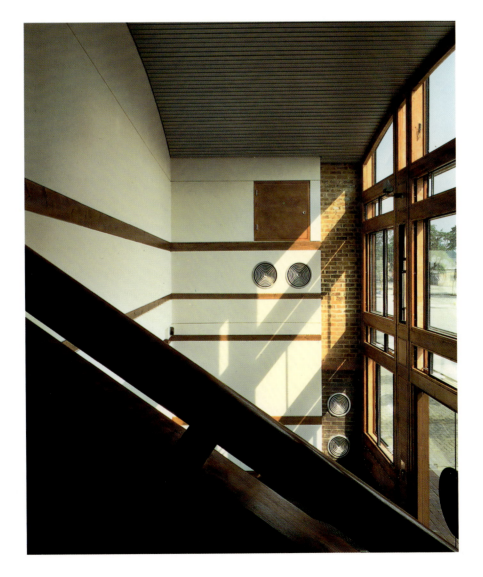

77

THE BEST IN INDUSTRIAL ARCHITECTURE

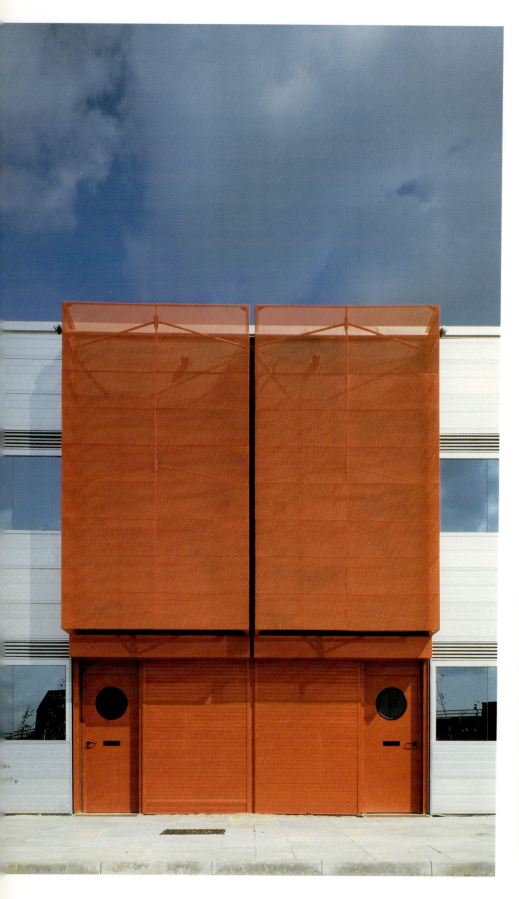

Speculative Factory Units

ARCHITECT: Jestico & Whiles, London, England
CLIENT: Trust Securities
FUNCTION OF BUILDING: Advanced factory units and offices
LOCATION: Waltham Cross, Hertfordshire, England
SIZE: 10,000m²
DATE OF COMPLETION: 1986
ARCHITECTURAL INTENTION: The design anticipates advances in building services and accommodates varying patterns of use. Incoming services are simply accessed and extended via an adapted truck roller shutter. Seamless glazing is glued in place like the flush windscreen of a car. With demountable cladding derived from a proprietary door system, the user is able to freely reorganize internal space to meet changing needs. The strong corrugations of the side elevations act as muscular book ends to the principal façade of the warehouse building. The pedestrian entrances are distinguished from the warehouse access doors by a brilliant red meshed cage resting lightly over paired port-holed doors.

THE BEST IN INDUSTRIAL ARCHITECTURE

Kensal Road Factories

ARCHITECT: John Outram Partnership, London, England
FUNCTION OF BUILDING: Light industrial factories
LOCATION: London, England
ARCHITECTURAL INTENTION: The row of factories at Kensal Road, London, has chosen to readdress the issue of street, as well as introduce symbols, allegory and narrative as devices to engage industrial buildings with the urban context, the user and the observer. At the street or urban level, the factories address the canal, and the public front, with calm elegance and classical exuberance respectively, stepping the buildings in pairs and allowing the sun to reinforce order and rhythm. On the public front the buildings are addressing the notion of street by the device of column, pediment and piano nobile which, together with a row of bollards marking the pavement we call conventional perceptions of road-building relationships.

The scaling of the buildings is sympathetic to its broader context, but via the 'classical' syntax also displays an architectural language that might be more easily read than the scales and forms normally associated with low cost industrial architecture. The architect's attention to detail, and careful ordering of materials, grain, texture and chiaroscuro, further provides a street architecture that can change in perspective, sunshine or rain, dependent upon the movement and empathy of the observer.

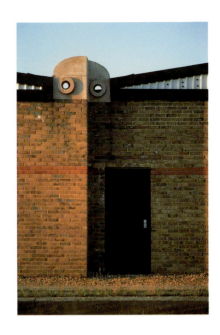

Kensal Road Factories continued over page

THE BEST IN INDUSTRIAL ARCHITECTURE

Kensal Road Factories continued

THE BEST IN INDUSTRIAL ARCHITECTURE

Kensal Road Factories continued

THE BEST IN INDUSTRIAL ARCHITECTURE

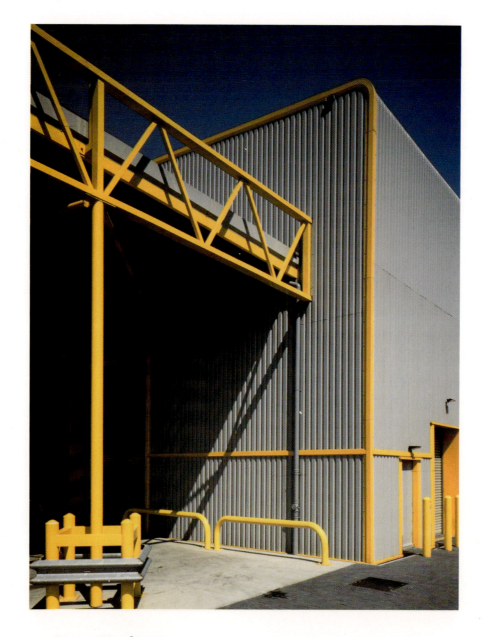

Paper Warehouse

ARCHITECT: Broadway Malyan, Reading, Berkshire, England

CLIENT: Hedsor Limited

FUNCTION OF BUILDING: Paper warehouse

LOCATION: Belvedere, Kent, England

SIZE: 6,225m^2

DATE OF COMPLETION: 1989

ARCHITECTURAL INTENTION: This paper warehouse has been designed to provide bays for Hedsor's bulk storage, cutting and distribution operations, with a capability for 50% future expansion. The building has a composite structure of pre-cast concrete columns and tie beams and steel lattice trusses with profiled metal roof sheeting. The tidal peat beneath Erith Marsh's subsoil required particular attention to substructive works.

SHEDS AND WAREHOUSES

Mothercare Distribution Centre

ARCHITECT: Conran Roche Architects, London, England

CLIENT: Mothercare UK

FUNCTION OF BUILDING: Distribution centre

LOCATION: Wellingborough, Northamptonshire, England

SIZE: 25,000m²

DATE OF COMPLETION: 1985–86

ARCHITECTURAL INTENTION: To provide storage volume of approximately 310,000m², enough for over three million garments. There are four levels of semi-automated racking in addition to conventional pallet racking, together with three-storey offices, staff and plant accommodation. In their naked form the huge skeletal stacking structure embraces a man-made canyon in which light transforms into the drama of a colossal stage set.

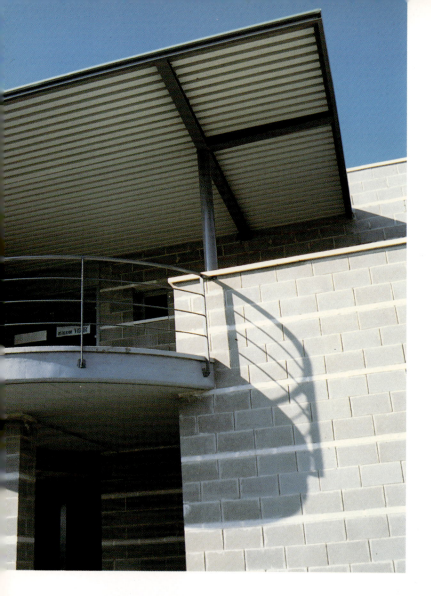

Igualada Commercial Factory Warehouse

ARCHITECT: Correa, Gallardo, Mannino, Arquitectos Asociados, Barcelona, Spain
CLIENT: Igualada Comercial
FUNCTION OF BUILDING: Factory, warehouse and offices
LOCATION: Barcelona, Spain
ARCHITECTURAL INTENTION: To provide a simple factory-warehouse within a controlled budget on a large site with three façades, a significant slope and non-orogonal geometry. Volume was controlled by fragmentation: the concrete block wall was the base; the high longitudinal windows became negative space; and the projecting roof was a floating plane which served as both roof and cornice.

The Grianan Building

ARCHITECT: Nicoll Russell, Dundee, Scotland
CLIENT: Scottish Development Agency and Dundee City Council
FUNCTION OF BUILDING: Technology Building
LOCATION: Dundee Technology Park, Dundee, Scotland
SIZE: 1,494m^2
DATE OF COMPLETION: 1988
ARCHITECTURAL INTENTION: The architecture derives from the relationship of two opposing technologies. The principal building comprises a steel frame of post and beam that is then locked into position by a simple masonry load bearing wall that anchors the composition to the ground and signifies the archaeology of the site.

THE BEST IN INDUSTRIAL ARCHITECTURE

Speculative Light Industrial Units

ARCHITECT: Richard Rogers Partnership, London, England
CLIENT: Speyhawk Land & Estates Ltd
FUNCTION OF BUILDING: Industrial units
LOCATION: Maidenhead, Berkshire, England
SIZE: 2,499m^2
DATE OF COMPLETION: 1985
ARCHITECTURAL INTENTION: Two speculative, light industrial units of 2,500 sq m each, with the potential to include variable amounts of office space to suit the demands of incoming tenants. The design intention was to create a high quality industrial building and ancillary office space with a practical and visual impact aimed towards advanced technology industries.

The building elements of transom, mullion, panel, extract fan, door and window have been composed within a modular system and stretched across the front of a series of dumb sheds like a painter's canvas across the utility of a softwood stretcher. Carefully cropped photographs can reduce this type of façadism into the parody of a De Stijl painting.

Laboratories

It was Louis Sullivan who proposed that 'form follows function'. Within the traditions of industrial architecture, the type of late twentieth century building which best tests this proposition is the laboratory building.

Dedicated to experiment, research and development, the complex programmes have excited architects to respond with buildings that are progressive, radical, often eccentric and usually at the forefront of contemporary technological innovation. The architecture of laboratory buildings often transcends style, with the best examples becoming icons of a Second Machine Age as well as symbols of a new functionalism.

At Sir Richard Rogers's Inmos building in Gwent, Wales, for example, the functional elements of structure, enclosure and services are visually articulated to clearly demonstrate how each is at the service of its function. The structure, a series of triangulated booms suspended from a centralized core, supports the light canopy of the roof which hovers over the external walls. This device declares a column-free interior and explains the requirement for flexibility and demountability. The heating, ventilation and air conditioning systems are stacked along the core structure, the size and complexity of these units clearly indicating a building of high climate control in the service of sophisticated technical operations. By the separation of structure, canopy and services, the enclosure is left as a modest system of gridded modular wall units that can be solid or glazed, depending on the context, orientation and function of the space they serve.

At Michael Hopkins's Schlumberger Building in Cambridge, England, an exoskeletal pylon structure restrains a fabric roof that is stretched as a tent to homogenize the principal, secondary and tertiary spaces below. Like the Inmos building, the system of space, structure and mechanics are both the servants of the programme and the symbol, where the symbol also submerges those systems to represent, at an implicit and abstract level, the philosophy of the company. The structure stands for geometry, precision and mathematics, the fabric for economy and fitness.

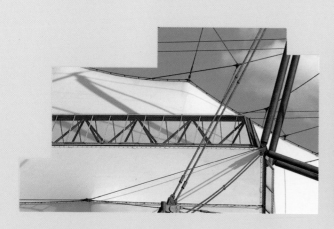

Ludwig Leo's Hydraulic Station and Lifeboat Station in Berlin were the progenitors of the new Functionalism. The value of the Machine Aesthetic, like a machine itself, is judged according to the fitness of form and structure to perform its function and the craft with which the elements comprising that form are made and brought together.

However, some architects subscribe to a view that the inside of a building – the private realm – has a duty to serve the internal functions alone and that the outside – the public realm – is a separate matter more concerned with content, public perception and cultural association. In the fragile environment of an historical community or within a natural landscape to which an advanced technological and scientific building type might appear alien, the internal spaces may, by necessity, subscribe to a language of stainless steel, servicing ducts, rubber doors and dust free surfaces of plastic and cellulose which are entirely legitimate to efficiency and operation. The outside however, with a greater duty to neighbourliness and the passer-by, is conceived as a façade and modelled in a manner or style that is at the service of either public consent or mandatory control.

Needless to say, arguments have persisted over the architectural and tectonic relationships of form and function. Some critics observe that form follows fashion and that with a few great exceptions (and each century has only a few great exceptions) all architects eventually fall victim to fashion by dressing their buildings in the fashion of the day, irrespective of function. This being the case we need to develop a hierarchy of critical awareness that can distinguish between the virtuoso's work that by its quality will always be beautiful irrespective of all other matters, and those other circumstances where modesty, ordinariness and popularism will enhance the public and private realm.

Inmos Microprocessor Factory

A building was required that provided office and ancillary space, as well as facilities for microchip wafer production. Speed of design and construction were critical factors.

A further constraint on the design of the building was the exceptionally high quality environmental control required by microchip production facilities. Air in the production area had to be absolutely clean to cut down on the failure rate of wafer production, a process minutely sensitive to dust.

The building design evolved as a single-storey structure conceived as a kit of rapidly erectible parts, with maximum off-site prefabrication to allow the building to be erected bay by bay.

The basic concept of Phase 1 of the building is a central linear circulation and service spine with internal wings for specialized activities. The spine 7.2m wide and 106m long, acts as an internal street or informal promenade, generous enough in size to contain vending machines, public telephones, seating, meeting places, planted areas and waiting areas for the offices. It provides total visual security control and is intended to link up with other future phases of building on the site, so that all the facilities in all the buildings are readily available to all staff.

Offices and restaurants are on the south side of the spine and the clean room production area to the north. The main air supply equipment is grouped in localized modules allowing minimum duct runs above the spine, ducts being taken across the roof to the point of use. Production wastes are collected in linear floor trenches and production supply services are distributed on service walls within the production zone. The layout of the building is infinitely extendible along the spine, with the ability to add on more of the 13 × 36m bays to the Newport site as required, with easy-access modular services additions.

An 8m bay scheme was proposed as the first phase of a 20 bay final development, set at the east end of the site so that the extension could take place in a westerly direction in the future as required. The very large clean room facility and shipping and receiving bays occupy the complete north side of the spine. The south side has one bay omitted, thus providing a landscaped courtyard offering daylight and sheltered open space between the offices and the restaurant.

CASE STUDY

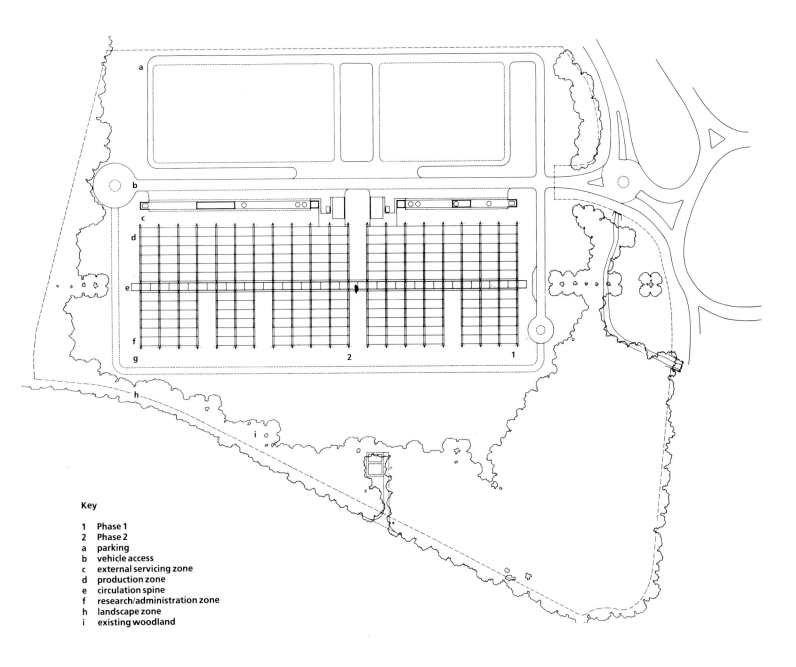

Key

1. Phase 1
2. Phase 2
a parking
b vehicle access
c external servicing zone
d production zone
e circulation spine
f research/administration zone
h landscape zone
i existing woodland

THE BEST IN INDUSTRIAL ARCHITECTURE

Inmos Microprocessor Factory

ARCHITECT: Richard Rogers Partnership, London, England

CLIENT: Inmos Ltd

FUNCTION OF BUILDING: Microprocessor factory

LOCATION: Newport, Gwent, South Wales

SIZE: 8,900m²

DATE OF COMPLETION: 1982

ARCHITECTURAL INTENTION:

Vestigial post-modern motifs seem out of place in this municipal building that is otherwise like its function, clean, clear, beautifully detailed and animated in its reflected light. Sir Richard Rogers' fetish for the declaration of structural and servicing systems reaches its apotheosis within the industrial building genre at Gwent in Wales, where a simple serviced shed is completely submerged by the orchestration of tanks, tubes, pylons, wires and ropes. This form of architectural language that has become known as hi-tech is a particularly English curiosity.

Inmos Microprocessor Factory *continued over page*

Inmos Microprocessor Factory continued

CASE STUDY

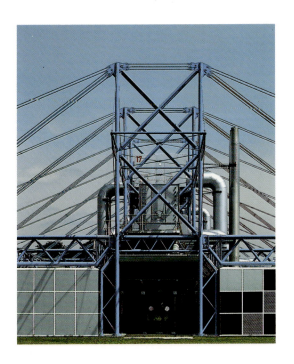

103

THE BEST IN INDUSTRIAL ARCHITECTURE

LABORATORIES

Braun Factory and Headquarters

ARCHITECT: James Stirling and Michael Wilford & Associates, London, England, in association with Walter Nägeli

CLIENT: Braun Company

FUNCTION OF BUILDING: Company headquarters and production

LOCATION: Melsungen, Germany

SIZE: 81,000m²

DATE OF COMPLETION: 1992 (first phase)

ARCHITECTURAL INTENTION: The industrial complex encompasses places of production, an administration building, stores, and a number of supplementary buildings, all arranged in a park landscape. The basic functional concept of the installation is to have different levels for various uses by layering upwards. The delivery roads for cars and lorries are directly on the site. Above this a pedestrian level is situated which connects the central car park to all areas of the production plant and which, because of the shape of the valley, always ends on the natural landscape. Above the footpaths is a level with an automatic transport ring between production area and store. Above all transport routes, high up in the green space are the production areas. The huge complex for Braun respects the functional tradition in form, materials and structure. Separate functions are distinguished by materials ranging from timber through concrete to lead and aluminium, while structures vary from post and beam frames to simple load-bearing elements.

Braun Medical Headquarters and Factory continued over page

THE BEST IN INDUSTRIAL ARCHITECTURE

Braun Medical Headquarters and Factory continued

LABORATORIES

Schlumberger Research Laboratory

ARCHITECT: Michael Hopkins and Partners, London, England
CLIENT: Schlumberger Group
FUNCTION OF BUILDING: Research centre
LOCATION: Cambridge, England
DATE OF COMPLETION: 1984
ARCHITECTURAL INTENTION: To provide a variety of types of space – private offices for individual study, open discussion areas for groups of scientists, laboratories, the Test Station – the hub of the building, the Winter Garden – a gathering place, restaurant and library for the whole centre. Although the scientists group into departments with their own identity, casual daily contact between departments is important for disseminating ideas. The Test Station and Winter Garden are placed in the centre of the building under a translucent membrane roof which makes a memorable sight on the Cambridge skyline. They are flanked on either side by two wings of study and laboratory accommodation.

The aesthetics of the Schlumberger building are dominated by the structural gymnastics of Ove Arup and Partners. A combination of steel masts, wire ropes and a translucent fabric canopy promotes a type of architectonic corsetry that the architect Michael Hopkins has employed on a number of occasions. In close up, the requirement for a complex hierarchy of structural support systems and tie-downs leads to a complex visual miscellany of wires and ropes that submerge any clear articulation of the building's function. At a distance, however, the same systems reveal themselves with a clarity and orderliness that has the building sat in its landscape and on the horizon with all the festivity of a circus marquee.

LABORATORIES

Schlumberger Research Centre continued over page

THE BEST IN INDUSTRIAL ARCHITECTURE

Schlumberger Research Centre continued

Nittokuno Research Center

ARCHITECT: Kisho Kurakawa, Tokyo, Japan
CLIENT: Nihon Tokushu Noyaku Seizo Co Ltd
FUNCTION OF BUILDING: Plant quanrantine centre
LOCATION: Yuki, Ibaraki, Japan
SIZE: 5,265m^2 approximately
DATE OF COMPLETION: 1986 (first phase)
ARCHITECTURAL INTENTION: This project is a scaled-down replica of another Kurakawa project built in Düsseldorf, Germany, for the Bayer Company. The Yuki research centre is only one twentieth the size of the as yet uncompleted German complex, but the aim was to employ the same basic design features and concepts.

The research block is three storeys in height. The top floor contains air conditioning apparatus while a control pit connected to the energy centre is located in the basement level. The most characteristic feature of this design is its pursuit of maximum flexibility to accommodate future research facilities.

The Nittokuno laboratory is a good example of a light industrial building uncertain of its tradition and unclear as to its future. The architecture, comprising post-modern motifs, industrial roofing systems over a concrete framed matrix, demonstrates the architectonic eclecticism that so often appears in the absence of a clearly defined theoretical position.

THE BEST IN INDUSTRIAL ARCHITECTURE

WMI Environmental Monitoring Laboratory

ARCHITECT: Perkins & Will, Chicago, Illinois, USA
CLIENT: Waste Management, Inc
FUNCTION OF BUILDING: Environmental monitoring laboratory
LOCATION: Geneva, Illinois, USA
SIZE: 13,900m^2
DATE OF COMPLETION: August 1988
ARCHITECTURAL INTENTION: To build 'the finest laboratory of its kind in the world' (following the client's wishes); the building's exterior design had to project a contemporary image, appropriate for the high-tech nature of a modern laboratory facility and reflective of the immaculate procedures required for ground water analyses. The design needed to relate aesthetically and environmentally to its rural context while maintaining a unique, identifiable and architecturally significant character. Four multi-flue chimneys anchor the composition of the environmental monitoring laboratory at Geneva, Illinois. A cut out in an otherwise pair of symmetrical lean-tos provides for two supporting columns and a canopy to mark the entrance via a single storey link block. The low lean-tos are anchored against a white brick and glass block building which with a neighbouring rotunda are distinguished by a sophisticated composition supported by elegant detailing.

LABORATORIES

PA Technology Center

ARCHITECT: Richard Rogers Partnership
CLIENT: PA Consulting Services Inc
FUNCTION OF BUILDING: Laboratory corporate facility
LOCATION: Princetown, New Jersey, USA
SIZE: 4,000m²
DATE OF COMPLETION: 1985
ARCHITECTRUAL INTENTION: The building had to express PA Technology's commitment to innovative technical research and be visible from a distance to the approaching visitor. Other requirements included maximum flexibility to permit further growth, a high level of freedom of circulation, flexibility in the arrangement of offices, labs and services. The design resulted in a very different structural solution to the inevitably comparable Inmos factory. Patscentre is on a smaller scale, there are less services to support between the masts. The span is 26m rather than 40m. The basic building concept is a central linear spine accommodating coffee shop, library and other communal activities. Open plan laboratories, offices and meeting rooms are located left and right of the top-lit spine. The single-storey suspended steel structure has at its base a portal frame which supports the dominating tubular A-Frame mast, from which are suspended standard steel section beams. Tie-down columns at the outer ends of these beams act in both tension and compression. The standard components formed a kit of parts prefabricated off site and were rapidly erected on site, bay by bay. Site welding was kept to a minimum and stainless steel pin connections were used wherever possible. The plant sits exposed, on suspended cradles connected with trusses to provide longitudinal stability for the A-Frames.

The PA Technology Center is identical in concept to Sir Richard Rogers' Inmos building at Gwent in Wales. The laboratory demands for column-free, flexible, internal environment, causes both the structure and the services to become exoskeletal, themselves submerging the silent shed with an aesthetic entirely derived from the engineer.

LABORATORIES

Research Laboratory for Experimental Traumatology

ARCHITECT: LOG ID, Tütingen, Germany
CLIENT: Professor Burri Foundation
FUNCTION OF BUILDING: Research laboratory
LOCATION: Ulm, Germany
SIZE: 690m²
DATE OF COMPLETION: 1988
ARCHITECTURAL INTENTION: The building was planned according to the principles of 'green solar architecture'. The core structure is a U-shaped, well-insulated massive building capable of storing heat energy; it houses the offices and laboratories. It is combined with a south-facing glasshouse containing the kitchen, auditorium and conference facilities. All rooms are located towards the glasshouse and contain large wall-to-wall folding doors so that solar energy can be efficiently used. Warm air from the glasshouse flows into the massive building when the folding doors are open. In addition, thermally regulated ventilators installed in the doors draw warm air into the offices. This means an energy saving of 10 to 40 per cent. The solar research laboratories are essentially a huge greenhouse wedged between two wings of cellular accommodation.

LABORATORIES

117

THE BEST IN INDUSTRIAL ARCHITECTURE

LABORATORIES

SZKFI Laboratory

ARCHITECT: István Janáky
CLIENT: Dunai Kóolajipari Vállalat/Duna Oil Company
FUNCTION OF BUILDING: Laboratory building
LOCATION: Szászhalombatta, Hungary
SIZE: 700m²
DATE OF COMPLETION: 1982
ARCHITECTURAL INTENTION: The plant of Hungarian Research and Development Institute for Hydrocarbon Industry is the central institution for the country's research activity in the field of oil industry. At the new plant, laboratory investigations and semi-operational experiments performed by the aid of models, take place. Most characteristic features of the architectonic design may be seen in the plant's layout, the five zones of buildings are surrounded by a network of ring roads. The SZKFI laboratories are arranged around a central ground level service road. Only single storey above ground the buildings drop into a pair of cuttings which connect under the service road at the sub-grade level. The decision to plant part of the building into the ground provides for the opportunity to locate a tented protective structure over the building's mechanical plant behind a vertical mud wall that establishes a dynamic contrast of materials, grains and textures.

LABORATORIES

Hooke Park College

ARCHITECT: Ahrends Burton and Koralek, London, England

CLIENT: The Parnham Trust

FUNCTION OF BUILDING: College for advanced manufacturing in wood

LOCATION: Dorset, England

SIZE: 600m²

DATE OF COMPLETION: 1990

ARCHITECTURAL INTENTION: The building is set in woodland near the School for Craftsmen in Wood at Parnham House. Three distinct types of building house the separate functions of the college – Workshop, Public Building, School Residences. They are integrated into the forest landscape. Each building form explores various structural solutions and utilises the properties of unsawn round timber in a new interpretation of timber technology. Public access is provided by an observation gallery over the Workshop which allows the public to view the processes of production and to pass through to the Public Interpretation Centre and Dining Room. The Public Building will also provide a focus in the forest for a system of walks and trails through the forest. The prototype incorporates the principal structural techniques, both tension and compress, developed for this project and was constructed under the direct supervision of this office.

Hooke Park College continued over page

THE BEST IN INDUSTRIAL ARCHITECTURE

LABORATORIES

Hooke Park College continued

The buildings at Hooke Park provide an opportunity to see architecture made as the singular and direct product of the act of construction. A series of timber sprung arches anchored to the landscape through a poured in-situ reinforced concrete base encloses a column free production space that synthesizes structure and construction to establish a true to the spirit of the woodworker's craft. The buildings seem to comprise material removed to create the clearing on which that building stands. And yet the double curved roof, port hole windows and joint technologies remind us that the installation is contemporary to properly serve the art of modern furniture production.

Municipal Architecture

There is a long history and fascinating partnership between good building and municipal works. It seems somehow that the engineering challenge of providing drinking water for five million people, or lighting thousands of buildings simultaneously, or disposing of seemingly endless masses of waste awakens the hero in the architect.

Not only that, but the sheer size of some endeavours and the eccentricity of form needed to accommodate complex engineering functions produces an architecture of richness and ironical ambiguity.

Even when the function appears to require no more than the most utilitarian of sheds to protect it from the weather, architectural polemics are explored to their limit, with virtuoso works of intellectual concentration that one would expect to see reserved for an Oxbridge Library or a Harvard Museum.

With a library or museum project, new processes of circulation and complex theories of art appreciation or library shelving and supervision will lead the architect to propose a new model within an established typology to which function and form can respond with either the originality of a new language or the eccentric reworking of an old. Either way, the architecture is in the hand of the architect, with the engineer as creative butler.

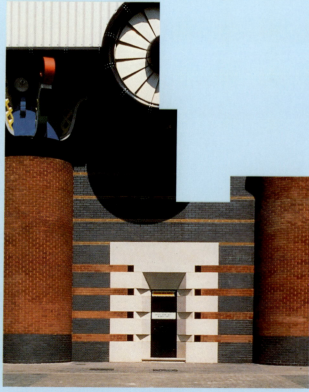

In municipal works, the opposite almost always obtains. The engineer will design the water pumps, sewerage settling tanks or recycling machinery and lay them out according to the precise technical requirements of their operation. The architect will then wrap the lot up, like a lady-in-waiting with a penchant for a particular style of clothes.

There are two notable exceptions. Michael Graves' Historical Center for Industry is a municipal building and a museum; as such, it is only just an industrial type but its architectonic quotations assign it to that category. The building's form refers to Sant' Elia's early drawings of an industrial city of the future; as a semiotic response to a building dedicated to the industry of the past, this is a witty inversion of historical precedent. Beyond that, it is a robust composition of muscular constructional elements that also recall the great Victorian engine rooms that symbolized the new age of mechanization, strength and stability in the nineteenth century. By contrast, Michel Kagan's Cité Technique makes an exquisite rearrangement of Corbusian syntax, submerging a series of modest functions beneath an heroic flourish of modernism to prove that, notwithstanding the brief, architecture has a duty to raise itself above the mere utility of construction. In this case, it becomes an icon of scholastic contemporaneity in the company of floating fire stations, sewerage works and water towers. Municipal works still promote themselves as fine architecture in the service of the public sector.

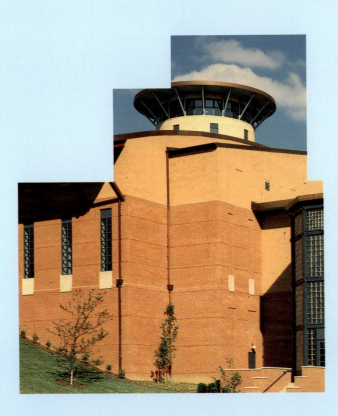

Cité Technique et Administrative

'The site chosen was a no-mans-land lacking in image and isolated from Paris by the Péripherique. On its longer side the site is parallel to the Péripherique. The northern façade is conceived as a bulwark, separating and protecting the building from the motorway. Responding to the problem of urbanizing an urban highway. Kagan proposed a series of industrial premises, perfectly aligned and separated from the péripherique by a green zone. It is a blueprint for a future megapolis, which will incorporate surrounding suburbs into the urban fabric of Paris by creating a series of coherent urban blocks.

The functional elements are arranged as a set of seemingly disparate objects around the sunny void of the courtyard, held in and unified by the hard rectangular edge of the ramparts.

Vehicular traffic is restricted to the courtyard/quay level from which access is gained to the garages in the two longer sides of the enclosure. The workshops are on the upper floors. The central building to the east accommodates the social activities. These three buildings are covered by a large billowing white wave, receding from the Péripherique in a form recalling that of the virgin site. This wave offers protection to the plant storage and nursery spaces and allows for their natural ventilation. To the west rises the narrow office tower, floating on pilotis and designed as two sliding planes which give the end walls a sleek silhouette. The movement of the staircase and the canopy give the façades an energy which permeates the entire scheme.

Axonometric from north east

CASE STUDY

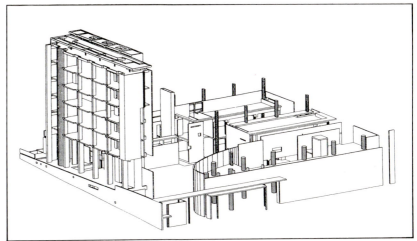

CASE STUDY

Cité Technique et Administrative

ARCHITECT: Michel W. Kagan, Paris, France
CLIENT: R.V.P./Ville de Paris
FUNCTION OF BUILDING: Technical and administrative centre for Parks and Gardens Department and Public Works Department of the city of Paris
LOCATION: Quai d'Ivry, Paris, France
SIZE: 9,000m²
DATE OF COMPLETION: June 1991
ARCHITECTURAL INTENTION: The project figure is a seductively simple square whose section tackles the problem of relating site boundaries at different levels by establishing a datum line. This reference becomes a "newly made ground" level associating existing levels one to another. The project layers are organized about this datum in a $\frac{above}{below}$ equation.

The white architecture of Le Corbusier's modernism has never ceased to influence and inspire architects of all generations throughout this century. Michel Kagan's Cité Technique confirms that with compositional scholarship the cubic syntax of early twentieth century reinforced concrete technology can be universal in its application and sublime in its manifestation, notwithstanding the relative humility of the building type. Kagan's building on the Paris Péripherique is accomplished enough to affirm that when architecture is at its most abstract it embraces the heroic qualities of immediacy and timelessness.

Cité Technique et Administrative continued over page

CASE STUDY

Cité Technique et Administrative continued

131

THE BEST IN INDUSTRIAL ARCHITECTURE

Water Control Towers

ARCHITECT: Cristian Cirici & Associates, Barcelona, Spain
CLIENT: FECSA
FUNCTION OF BUILDING: Control and regulation of water flow
LOCATION: Lago de Estangento, Pirineo de Lerida, Spain
SIZE: 40m² each tower
ARCHITECTURAL INTENTION: The twin towers were built to control the flow of water in and out of the reservoir, by means of two 3.50m diameter pipes that join Lake Estangento and the *Central Hidraúlica Reversible de Sollente* 16km away on the coast.

The upper part of each gate-tower houses electrical components and the control room. This space is lit through a dome opening. Access to the control room is through a spiral staircase attached to the tower. The hydraulic pump that moves the gates extends over the building and is protected by a stainless-steel, central-heated cage.

MUNICIPAL ARCHITECTURE

THE BEST IN INDUSTRIAL ARCHITECTURE

Water Treatment Centre

ARCHITECT: Terry Farrell and Company, London, England
CLIENT: Thames Water Authority
FUNCTION OF BUILDING: Sewerage treatment and water supply
LOCATION: Reading, Berkshire, England
SIZE: Ground floor: 1,465m²; total floor areas: 2,005m²
DATE OF COMPLETION: June 1982
ARCHITECTURAL INTENTION: Apart from all the underground tanks and water treatment plant, facilities were required in this building for workers who maintain other installations in the area; these included laboratories, cafeterias, stores, workshops, offices and a computer room. In addition, a centrally-placed visitors' centre was included to inform the public of the authorities' operations. The building straddles an enormous treatment tank set into the ground and containing several million gallons of water; weight and stability are provided by the above-ground building.

The skilfully detailed Thames Water Authority building conceals a relatively complex interior that is rich in colour and metaphor and animated by a cascade of natural lighting vaults. The architectural experience enjoyed by the arrangement of structure, fabric, light, colour and texture leaves the two post-modern columns as vestigial and gratuitous gestures.

Thames Water Authority Headquarters continued over page

THE BEST IN INDUSTRIAL ARCHITECTURE

Thames Water Authority Headquarters continued

MUNICIPAL ARCHITECTURE

Blueprint Park

ARCHITECT: Thorpe Architecture, Arundel, Sussex
CLIENT: British Gas (Southern) plc
FUNCTION OF BUILDING: Production/distribution units
LOCATION: Blueprint Park, Hilsea, Portsmouth, England
SIZE: 25,000m² approximately
DATE OF COMPLETION: 1991
ARCHITECTURAL INTENTION: To provide relatively simple, economic enclosures, sophisticated by both proportion and attention to detail. 'Slick sheds' gleam on the horizon and bold profiled horizontal cladding orchestrated by limited amounts of both glazed screened sheds and external structural elements. The visual weight of the Hilsea gas station is relieved at the corners by a stepped cut out that exposes the line of ectoskeletal columns that support the principal facade. A detailed junction between column head and canopy reveals a close attention to detailing that with fine workmanship creates an extremely distinguished building.

Blueprint Park continued over page

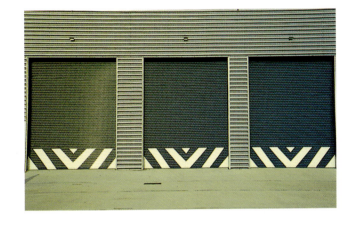

THE BEST IN INDUSTRIAL ARCHITECTURE

Blueprint Park continued

MUNICIPAL ARCHITECTURE

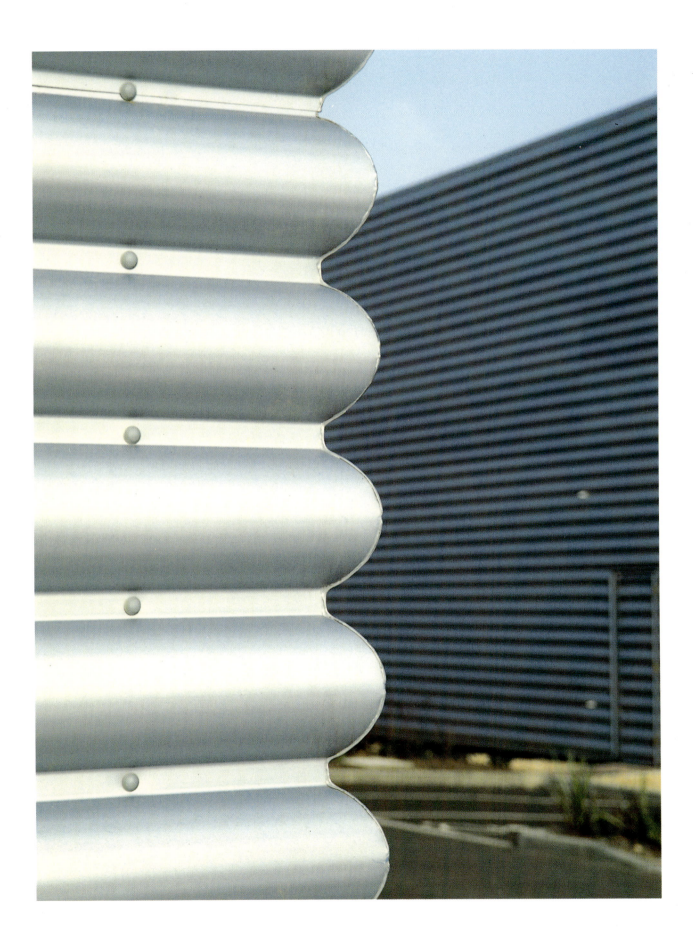

THE BEST IN INDUSTRIAL ARCHITECTURE

MUNICIPAL ARCHITECTURE

Recycling Plant for Domestic Waste

ARCHITECT: Astrup og Hellern, Oslo, Norway
CLIENT: Resirkuleringsanlegget i Oslo A/S and Oslo Lysverker
FUNCTION OF BUILDING: Recycling of waste to generate power
LOCATION: Oslo, Norway
SIZE: 21,500m^2
DATE OF COMPLETION: 1989
ARCHITECTURAL INTENTION: To create a recycling plant to use domestic waste as a fuel to generate electricity. The building design has to reconcile the function of waste arrival, the recycling process and power generation. From the air the recycling complex appears as an unwelcome visitor to the countryside outside Oslo. But the recycling plant, heavy machinery and processing equipment hide behind monolithic screens and curtain walls, whose architecture is great care and craftsmanship.

THE BEST IN INDUSTRIAL ARCHITECTURE

MUNICIPAL ARCHITECTURE

Tottenham Hale Station

ARCHITECT: William Alsop and John Lyall, London, England

CLIENT: British Rail (Network Southeast)

FUNCTION OF BUILDING: Rail interchange station

LOCATION: Tottenham Hale, London

DATE OF COMPLETION: February 1992

ARCHITECTURAL INTENTION: The design gives a new identity to the station, and confers a sense of arrival for air travel passengers and existing customers. It achieves this with a simple steel structure spanning the tracks, from which are suspended the overhead electrification cables, information signs, lights and glass 'valances' which protect the covered platforms from driving rain. This gives a clear open feel to the station platforms themselves, ensuring good visibility through the station when trains are coming in and making it a safe environment for people on their own especially at night. The track is spanned by an elegant steel and glass footbridge served by an escalator and stairs which discharge passengers into the ticket hall of the London Transport Station. The simple steel framed white gridded box of the Tottenham Hale Station in London is relieved by a curved single-storey lobby building.

THE BEST IN INDUSTRIAL ARCHITECTURE

MUNICIPAL ARCHITECTURE

Natural Gas Purification Plant

ARCHITECT: Hamminga & Haverkort BV, Emmen, Netherlands
CLIENT: Nederlandse Aardolie Maatschappij b.v.
FUNCTION OF BUILDING: Natural gas purification plant
LOCATION: Emmen, Netherlands
SIZE: 4,000m^2
DATE OF COMPLETION: 1987
ARCHITECTRUAL INTENTION: It is impossible to disguise this building, or bury it by camouflage in the landscape; at night, safety regulations demand that it is lit up. Therefore the solution was to use a unifying 'factory aesthetic'. The plant is highly technical, and so the processing buildings follow function foremost. To unify the site, the non-factory elements – offices, canteen, shops, petrol station – followed the same style as the technical buildings, the round shape of the canteen reflecting the round shape of the laboratory.

The plant is resolved in composite by a works canteen that reduces the scale of the building as it meets the water. The circular pavilion structure is comfortable enough on the water, leaving the support pylons as rather gratuitous structural elements.

THE BEST IN INDUSTRIAL ARCHITECTURE

MUNICIPAL ARCHITECTURE

Historical Center of Industry and Labor

ARCHITECT: Michael Graves Architect, Princeton, New Jersey, USA
CLIENT: Ohio Historical Society
FUNCTION OF BUILDING: Museum, research center, archives and classrooms
LOCATION: Youngstown, Ohio, USA
SIZE: 11,000m^2 approximately
DATE OF COMPLETION: 1986
ARCHITECTURAL INTENTION: To provide a facility devoted to the study and presentation of the industrial history of the Mahoning River Valley. The building's elements represent forms typical of the American industrial landscape. The character is derived not so much from recently built steel mills as from the extremely potent images of nineteenth century industrial examples.

The Historical Center for Industry is strangely reminiscent in built form of the progressive drawings by Sant'Elia during his brief career as a leading futurist architect. Whether premeditated or not the references are more than appropriate for a building dedicated to the history of industrial heritage.

MUNICIPAL ARCHITECTURE

Storm Water Pumping Station

ARCHITECT: John Outram Partnership
FUNCTION OF BUILDING: Pumping station
LOCATION: Isle of Dogs, London, England
ARCHITECTURAL INTENTION: It is said that every century has its classical revival, England is seeing its second toward the end of the twentieth century and no more eccentrically expressed than in the complex architectural language of John Outram. The London pumping station on the Isle of Dogs, where the seemingly eclectic mixture of materials laid about a pediment of sitting over two over scaled columns is a rich allegorical confection that was seen to have more to do with the author's private and intellectual world of fable and fantasy than with the functions of pumping water.

149

THE BEST IN INDUSTRIAL ARCHITECTURE

MUNICIPAL ARCHITECTURE

Sewage Pumping Station

ARCHITECT: Björn Hallsson
CLIENT: Reykjavik City
FUNCTION OF BUILDING: Sewage Pumping Station
LOCATION: Reykjavik, Iceland
DATE OF COMPLETION: 1989
ARCHITECTURAL INTENTION: The Icelandic sewerage works complex is a beautiful arrangement of buildings in the landscape. The grass battered walls are offered up to the building's perimeter, reminiscent of an ancient settlement watched over by the benign eye of the cubic belvedere that marks the centre of the composition. In its abstraction the small building complex is a fine testimonial to the harmony of modern architecture and profane landscapes.

THE BEST IN INDUSTRIAL ARCHITECTURE

Majadahonda Water Purification Plant

ARCHITECT: Iniki Abalos and Juan Herreros, Madrid, Spain
CLIENT: Communidad Autonoma de Madrid
LOCATION: Majadahanda, Madrid, Spain
DATE OF COMPLETION: 1988
ARCHITECTURAL INTENTION: To reconcile the technical dictates of water purification with the administrative needs of a public works building. The building is a simple yet robust composition of elemental forms, some of which break out of the principal façade to establish an eccentricity in counterpoint to the corrugated curved roof, spanning the major hall.

THE BEST IN INDUSTRIAL ARCHITECTURE

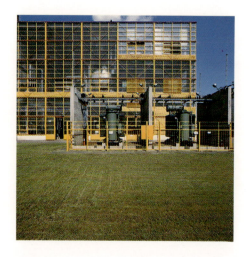

MUNICIPAL ARCHITECTURE

Incineration Plant

ARCHITECT: Antal Lázár, A&D Studio, Budapest, Hungary
CLIENT: City of Budapest
FUNCTION OF BUILDING: Incineration plant
LOCATION: Budapest, Hungary
DATE OF COMPLETION: 1981
ARCHITECTURAL INTENTION: To provide an incineration plant to deal with waste from one million residents. A daily 1200t of waste is incinerated without harming the environment: the resulting energy is used to generate electricity for heat and light. To build the plant quickly, the architects chose a solution that needed little on-site assembly. The foundations were poured on site, with columns and beams being constructed in steel. The building concept was based on defining the variable interior space with vast, rapidly mountable elements. The architects must have been tempted to provide companions for the sculpture and chimney that mark the site of this incineration plant by dislocating the functional elements and arranging them in the landscape. In the event the plant is collected and caged in a yellow gridded structure, part of which jumps over the perimeter fence to create a signpost for the complex.

THE BEST IN INDUSTRIAL ARCHITECTURE

MUNICIPAL ARCHITECTURE

Exhaust Purification Plant

ARCHITECT: 4B Arkitekter A/S, Oslo, Norway
CLIENT: Oslo Cleaning Department, Renholdsverket
FUNCTION OF BUILDING: Purification plant
LOCATION: Brobekkveien, Oslo, Norway
SIZE: 800m^2
DATE OF COMPLETION: 1989
ARCHITECTURAL INTENTION: To provide a purification plant that shows a conscious use of materials and formal grammar, which bring order to a diverse industrial complex. The plant is one of the main places in Oslo where rubbish is collected. This extension is to clean the smoke and gases from the burning process. The functional requirements of the exhaust purification plant promotes a complex arrangement of cylinders, chimneys, cubic boxes and ventilating lanterns that without any self-conscious idiomatic device makes an architecture of great beauty.

THE BEST IN INDUSTRIAL ARCHITECTURE

MUNICIPAL ARCHITECTURE

Cable Storage Plant

ARCHITECT: István Janáky, IPARTERV, Budapest, Hungary
CLIENT: Hungarian Post Office
FUNCTION OF BUILDING: Cable storage
LOCATION: Budaörs, Hungary
SIZE: 25,000m²
DATE OF COMPLETION: 1990
ARCHITECTURAL INTENTION: The architectural shape of the plant deliberately diverges from the general location of industrial objects, because the three large buildings (storehouse-workshop, high capacity storage and printing works) represent three different kinds of architectural character regarding construction, materials and detail. The ensemble character of the building-group is ensured by careful location.

THE BEST IN INDUSTRIAL ARCHITECTURE

MUNICIPAL ARCHITECTURE

Lambeth River Station

ARCHITECT: William Alsop and John Lyall, London, England (Project Architect Peter Clash)
CLIENT: London Fire and Civil Defence Authority
FUNCTION OF BUILDING: Floating fire station
LOCATION: Lambeth Bridge, Thames, London
SIZE: 400m^2
ARCHITECTURAL INTENTION: To replace existing facilities for the fireboats used by the London Fire and Civil Defence Authority at Lambeth Bridge. The new fire station involved the construction of a completely new floating structure. Plant rooms, workshops, locker rooms, a gymnasium and a lecture room are housed within the steel hull. A lightweight steel-framed aluminium clad structure contains dormitory accommodation, showers, offices and mess room/kitchen. Architecturally the scheme achieves a long low horizontal profile emphasised by silver profiled cladding system to the superstructure, painted black in order to lose the bulk against the water.

MUNICIPAL ARCHITECTURE

Pumphouse, Royal Victoria Dock

ARCHITECT: Richard Rogers Partnership, London, England

CLIENT: London Dockland Development Corporation

FUNCTION OF BUILDING: Pumping station

LOCAtION: London, England

SIZE: 850m² (above ground)

ARCHITECTURAL INTENTION: The provision of a water pumping station at the confluence of new, deep underground channels, to lift waste water up to a high level for discharge into the River Thames.

The East London pumping station is a powerful composition of cylinders, amplified by strong washes of colour and edged with guard rails and balustrades. There is a conspicuous absence of expressed structure, normally typical of Rogers' work, which is ironic given that a pumping station would imply an honest revelation of its mechanics. Any aesthetic eccentricity is reserved for a series of boundary light fittings that hang over the edge of the building like the probisci of a giant insect.

THE BEST IN INDUSTRIAL ARCHITECTURE

Water Purification Plant

ARCHITECT: Alfredo Lozano Gardel, Madrid, Spain
CLIENT: Integral Water Planning of Madrid (P.I.A.M.)
FUNCTION OF BUILDING: Water purification plant
LOCATION: Pinilla, Madrid, Spain
DATE OF COMPLETION: 1992
ARCHITECTURAL INTENTION: A solid masonry base, perforated with small port hole windows and elegant access doors supports an upper storey fenestration system that implies a colonnade of pilasters resting under a simple pitched roof. The modest composition and simple expression of culturally understandable architectural elements that derive from history but don't imitate it, converts the brief for the Pinilla Valley project into a fine piece of architecture.

MUNICIPAL ARCHITECTURE

Water Purification Plant

ARCHITECT: Alfredo Lozano Gardel, Madrid, Spain
CLIENT: Integral Water Planning of Madrid (P.I.A.M.)
FUNCTION OF BUILDING: Water purification plant
LOCATION: Buitrago, Madrid, Spain
DATE OF COMPLETION: 1987
ARCHITECTURAL INTENTION: The Buitrago del Lozoya project is a beautifully crafted assembly of new and old materials. The random stonework anchors the building to the ground and stabilizes a composition of lattice, perforated and solid steel frameworks. The juxtaposition of structural technology and the ordinariness of load-bearing materials creates aesthetic juxtapositions of engaging complexity.

THE BEST IN INDUSTRIAL ARCHITECTURE

Power Station Offices

ARCHITECT: Architect Geir Grung A/S, arch.MNAL Geir Grung, arch.MNAL Mahendra Aindley, arch.Christina Dumitrescu and arch.MNAL Finn Hannestad, Asker, Norway

CLIENT: Aktieselskabet Tyssefaldene

FUNCTION OF BUILDING: Offices for a power company

LOCATION: Tyssedal, Hardanger, Norway

SIZE: 1,500m^2

DATE OF COMPLETION: 1988

ARCHITECTURAL INTENTION: The Norwegian fjords on the west coast very often seem to dig right in the mountains. Steep hills on both sides offer few possibilities for making roads or putting up buildings. When the new power station was built right into the mountain, the old building became cold and distant. However, the power company's need for more offices could be combined with the authority's wish to preserve the old building. The old generator building is now a museum, and an outstanding example of the successful combination of refurbishment and preservation.

MUNICIPAL ARCHITECTURE

Comestibles The food and drink industry is one of the richest and largest in the world and yet the level of architectural patronage is small compared to that of, for example, manufacturing or municipal works.

It would seem that the great bread manufacturers, chocolate makers and meat processing multinationals do not believe in the dictum that good architecture is good business. To many comestible giants, function is optimized by the systems engineer, the shed is fashioned by the lowest-bid design-and-build contractor and the colour of the cladding is decided by the outcome of a local high school competition.

All of which is a great loss, when one considers that the utilitarian programme for a sewerage works can inspire a good piece of architecture. It takes little imagination to grasp the potential of a hamburger works or a flour mill in the hands of a great architect. The process of taking in corn and putting out bread, or of packaging sides of beef into neat little discs of frozen steaklets is rich in the opportunities for surreal juxtaposition as can be shown by the Norwegian dairy by LBR, where the conventional idea of a milk bottle has been treated like a Claes Oldenburg sculpture and enlarged to a scale that is simultaneously familiar and unfamiliar. Indeed with artists collaborating on comestible architecture – especially globally important foodstuffs – the combination of the iconography of the raw product with the symbol of its metamorphosis to the end product could make factories for edibles such as streaky bacon or smoked salmon become as famous as their makers or make their makers famous. The American architects SITE, led by James Wines, have explored the overlap between sculpture installation art and architecture to build a chain of extraordinary warehouses that have brought the mail order company BEST to the attention of a worldwide audience.

It could be said that Philippe Starck's *Flamme d'Or* on top of the Asahi Brewery and Beer Hall in Japan is a move towards art-architecture, but the huge illuminated blob is both wilful and gratuitous and misses the opportunity to make a sculptural-tectonic response to the universal phenomenon of beer drinking.

In fact, most of the comestible factories are orthodox in both concept and realization; even Michael Graves' winery in Napa Valley combines the historicist-academic tradition, with precedent and reference to make an arcadian collection of post-modern buildings that become more self-regarding and idiomatic than abstract symbols of the culture of wine. Style like post-modernism is difficult to avoid, especially when critics are keen to make life easier by demanding that everything can and should be categorized. But when this is achieved either by the unselfconscious utilitarianism and archaic buildings methods of a Chinese grape drying tower, or by the beautifully crafted brewery for Farsons, the form of which is dictated by the demands of climate control, it is apparent that although fine art may have a role in support of good building, architecture can triumph without it.

THE BEST IN INDUSTRIAL ARCHITECTURE

Simonds Farson Cisk Brewery

Cooling is the main environmental task performed by the building. The maintenance of comfortable conditions for staff in the process hall reduces the cooling load associated with the brewing process, which operates at approximately 2 degrees centigrade. The architect's strategy is to enclose the process hall within a 'jacket' – a space which acts as a buffer between the ball and the external environment – so that the only surface of the hall which is exposed externally is the roof.

At night the solar radiation absorbed earlier by the roof is re-radiated into the process hall. The thermal capacity of the roof construction has been adjusted so that this does not occur until cool night air is available for ventilation. Within the upper part of the hall, naturally-rising warm air is directed by the shape of the roof into the south tower, to exit via the windows. Cool night air is simultaneously drawn through high-level windows in the walls separating the process hall from the jacket. At all times the air in the lower part of the process hall, where the brewery plant and staff are located, remains at a comfortable temperature without mechanical ventilation or cooling.

The form of the building stems from the environmental strategy and provides a distinctive roofline. The architects rejected the idea of maintaining a consistent section and have treated the ventilation towers as rooftop pavilions architecturally integrated with the north and south façades. The architectural treatment is derived from traditional Maltese baroque architecture, but the clarity of the architectural strategy has not always been carried through in the details of the limestone construction.

The external treatment is not carried into the interior. In the process hall, tiling and brightly painted steelwork decorate and brighten the space but they are upstaged by the carefully arranged and beautifully detailed stainless steel brewing equipment. In the circulation spaces within the jacket, plain walls, metal gratings and pipework predominate, giving a surprisingly industrial character.

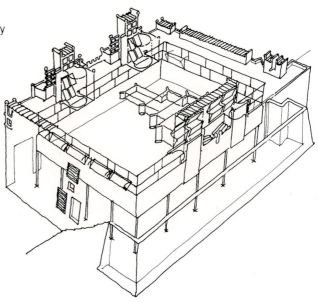

CASE STUDY

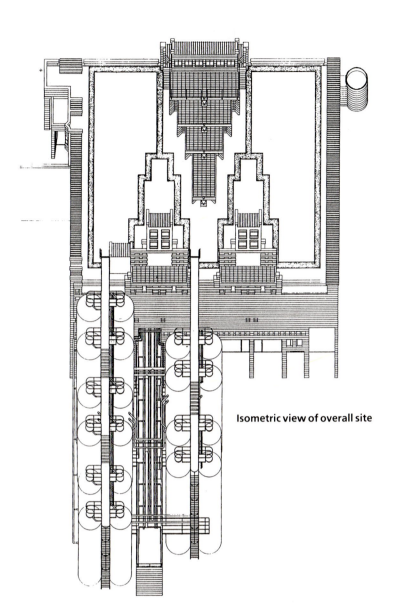

Isometric view of overall site

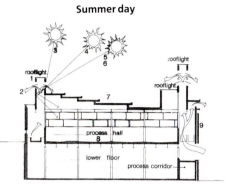

Summer day

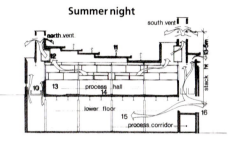

Summer night

171

THE BEST IN INDUSTRIAL ARCHITECTURE

Simonds Farson Cisk Brewery

ARCHITECT: Alan Short and Brian Ford of Peake Short & Partners

CLIENT: Simonds Farson Cisk Brewery, Malta

FUNCTION OF BUILDING: Brewery process building, housing fermentation, filtration and yeast propagation equipment

LOCATION: Mriehel, Malta

SIZE: 2,500m²

DATE OF COMPLETION: July 1990

ARCHITECTURAL INTENTION: The conventional prototypes for new brewery buildings were devised in America and Western Europe, steel framed, corrugated metal clad sheds, all air-conditioned, very inappropriate for the lower latitudes. Our building is the complete inverse, made of massive limestone, detailed according to long-established good masonry practice, controlling its internal environment quite naturally using stack effect ventilation induced at nighttime by the judicious opening and closing of windows, consuming virtually no energy. Measured results are excellent, better than predicted in our original computer predictions. The complex problems of production and climate have been solved with great technological skill that also allows the building to explore an architectural vocabulary that simultaneously relates the building to its landscape, establishes a monumentality and effects scale changes that occasionally sees the building as being intimate and directly responsive to the human scale. Although the steelwork and stonework would seem to be in direct competition, the quality of direct and reflected light tends to homogenize the composition bringing opposing elements into harmony. The care in detailing both the level of the general and the specific supposes an act of faith by the client that is welcomed but rare.

Simonds Farson Cisk Brewery continued over page

Simonds Farson Cisk Brewery continued

CASE STUDY

Simonds Farson Cisk Brewery continued over page

THE BEST IN INDUSTRIAL ARCHITECTURE

Dairy

ARCHITECT: LBR, v/Peter Collett Jorgensen, MNAL, Oslo, Norway
CLIENT: Ostlands Meieriet
FUNCTION OF BUILDING: Dairy
LOCATION: Sem, Vestfold, Norway
SIZE: 8,300m^2
DATE OF COMPLETION: August 1989
ARCHITECTURAL INTENTION: To create a dairy with an optimal logistic solution, adjusting the building to the landscape, and also allowing the building to manifest itself as a production plant.

The huge milk churns signify the function of the building as well as animating its form. The lorry suckling on the milky white mechanical udders is an amusing industrialized simile to the calf and the mother cow.

Trebor Sweet Factory

ARCHITECT: Arup Associates, London, England
CLIENT: Trebor Limited
FUNCTION OF BUILDING: New manufacturing buildings, amenities and warehouse
LOCATION: Colchester, Essex
SIZE: 9,400m²
DATE OF COMPLETION: 1980
ARCHITECTURAL INTENTION: To develop a master plan for the site and design new buildings with an awareness of how the quality of the working environment is as important as the functional requirements of the manufacturing process. The design reflects the client's wish that each part of the factory should have a separate identity and not merely be rationalized into one large shed.

Arup Associates' factory site as a backdrop to a series of single-storey, hatted pavilions pinned to the ground by a pair of service chimneys and acting as a tectonic fence to the surrounding farmland.

THE BEST IN INDUSTRIAL ARCHITECTURE

The Clos Pegase Winery

ARCHITECT: Michael Graves, Architect, Princeton, New Jersey, USA

CLIENT: The Clos Pegase Winery

FUNCTION OF BUILDING: To house winery, offices and owner's private residence

LOCATION: Calistoga, California, USA

ARCHITECTURAL INTENTION: To provide a winery with public winetasting facilities, private winemaking functions, a residence for the owner and a sculpture park. The winery and residence were completed, but plans for the sculpture park were suspended. The master plan organized the site along an axis of water emanating from 'the grotto of Pegasus' and concluding in two formal ponds. Private and public areas are separated by the line of the axis.

Michael Graves' winery in Napa Valley, California, is an eclectic collection of architectural languages each making reference to historical precedents that are in term relevant to the history of wine. The soft stuccoed materials and precise architectural modelling throw shadows across the complex arrangement of buildings to amplify the articulation of solid and void and secure an architectural response to the strong Californian sunlight.

The Clos Pegase Winery continued over page

COMESTIBLES

THE BEST IN INDUSTRIAL ARCHITECTURE

The Clos Pegase Winery continued

Draught Beer Racking Plant

ARCHITECT: Michael Hopkins and Partners, London, England
CLIENT: Greene King breweries
LOCATION: Bury St Edmunds, Suffolk, England
SIZE: 1,100m² approximately
DATE OF COMPLETION: 1980
ARCHITECTURAL INTENTION: A sensitive planning situation had to be overcome and the scheme is designed to respond to existing field patterns retaining streams and hedgerows, and historic water meadows once used for dray horses. A masterplan has been prepared for future long term needs and expansion.

The building is very highly serviced and the design involved close collaboration with the Client. The layout of the production plant and services has been organized to provide a disciplined frame work for future alterations and expansions.

THE BEST IN INDUSTRIAL ARCHITECTURE

Asahi Brewery and Beer Hall

ARCHITECT: Phillippe Starck

CLIENT: Asahi Brewing Company

FUNCTION OF BUILDING: Brewery and Beer Hall

LOCATION: Tokyo, Japan

DATE OF COMPLETION: 1990

ARCHITECTURAL INTENTION: *La Flamme D'Or* that crowns the Beer Hall of the Asahi brewery building in Tokyo is a mysterious symbol for the Japanese beer industry. Out of scale with the supporting building the flame nevertheless has a citywide presence that will have enough power in its abstraction to seduce the new beer drinking population of Japan.

Grape Drying Towers, Turfan, China

Rebuilt on the walls of a crumbling settlement, the clay grape vine-fruit drying towers are beautiful in their simplicity of construction, fitness of materials and modesty of form. Handmade and homemade these multi-level factories are somewhere near to what Frank Lloyd Wright called the zero degree of architecture; where architecture starts without architects and construction is only one step beyond the cave.

Transferable Language

In *The Classical Language of Architecture*, Sir John Summerson describes classicism as a language of architecture. By that he meant that its component parts – for example base, column, capital, entablature and pediment – can be compared to words, and that the skills required in their arrangement to comprise a building are the same as those needed to master the rules of grammar and syntax for the construction of a sentence or paragraph.

In architectural criticism as well as education the beauty of a building may be judged on many things, but never without reference to architectural vocabulary. The skill is in selecting and composing those materials, so that when brought together they serve their function optimally to declare the author's intention clearly and succinctly. Consequently, architecture has some universal principles in the same way that every human language has rules of grammar for it to be understood. By education the language is learned and with constant practice a fluency may be reached that will allow for experiment. A scholar of classical Greek architecture, for example, might feel that its principles are so universal that its archetypal building, the temple, is merely the starting point for a language that can be transferred to town halls, schools, hospitals, housing – indeed any and every other building type. Although almost every century since the demise of the Greco-Roman empires has seen a classical revival, the increasing distance of each one from its heritage establishes an architectonic anachronism that is in danger of self-parody.

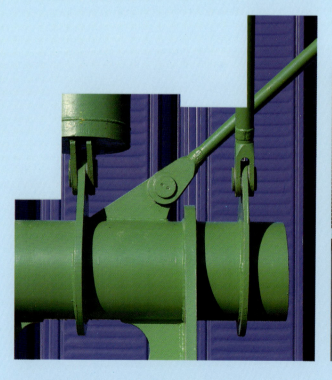

So architects enthusiastic about *zeitgeist* and contemporaneous issues belonging to the twentieth century saw the Deutscher Werkbund and the English Arts and Craft tradition as an opportunity to create a new language using the machine as its grammatical matrix. Because the machine offers a great variety of form, architects have found an escape from the pedagogy of classical ideas to practise a language that can respect the theories of functionalism while declaring an individuality particular to the phenomenology of type and place. Before form, perhaps inside form, there is a structure or group of structures that creates function; like the wings of an aeroplane or the keel of a boat, when the structural relationship is working optimally the object pleases the eye. An ocean-going yacht is a machine for sailing in wherein the beauty of the machine increases *pro rata* to the fitness of its structure to perform its function.

If this idea is transferred to the factory type where the elegance of much recent industrial architecture relies on a form derived from the rationalism of an articulated structure and services, then it is inevitable that intellectual curiosity will seek to explore the language of the Machine Aesthetic across as many building types as possible.

J. Sainsbury Supermarket and Housing Development

The development is on the site of what was a large bakery which, when demolished, left a complete urban block to be rebuilt. The desire to achieve an uninterrupted flexible space in the supermarket led to a fresh approach to the design, more akin to the traditional 'market hall'. The structure is therefore clearly expressed and is used to generate the form and appearance of the building. The relationship of the development to the surrounding buildings was an important aspect of the design concept, and so the articulated structure of the supermarket is on a 6m grid to fit in with the rhythm of the party walls of the listed houses opposite.

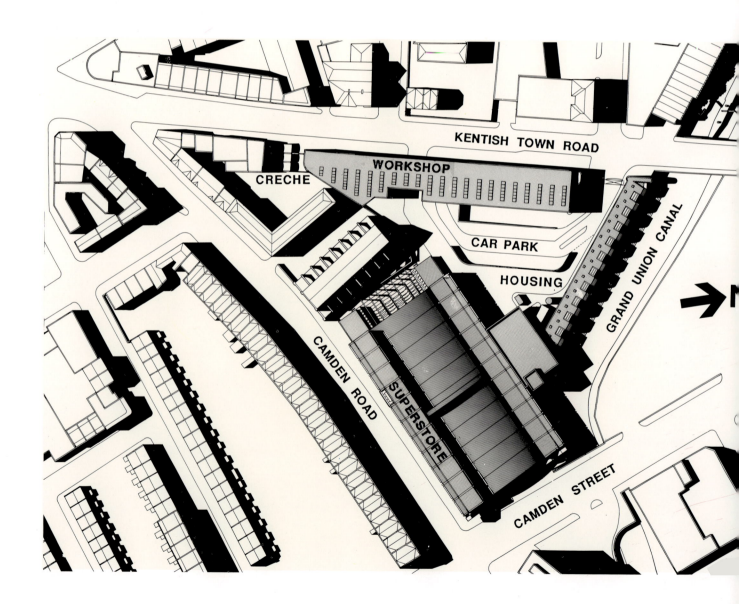

CASE STUDY

195

THE BEST IN INDUSTRIAL ARCHITECTURE

Supermarket and Housing

ARCHITECT: Nicholas Grimshaw & Partners, London, England

CLIENT: J. Sainsbury plc

FUNCTION OF BUILDING: Supermarket, crèche, workshops, canal-side housing and car park

LOCATION: London, England

DATE OF COMPLETION: 1988

ARCHITECTURAL INTENTION: While most large supermarkets in England are dressed with timber and tiles to resemble huge medieval barns, Nicholas Grimshaw has been loyal to the machine aesthetic in building a supermarket for Sainsbury's in London that is quite properly a factory for selling food. If it is not surprising that the systems of industrial buildings transfer easily to this urban retail outlet, then it might be more so that the same language feels at home in a row of terraced houses built by the same architect as an adjunct to the overall development.

J. Sainsbury Supermarket continued over page

THE BEST IN INDUSTRIAL ARCHITECTURE

J. Sainsbury Supermarket continued

TRANSFERABLE LANGUAGE

Nantes Centre Commercial

ARCHITECT: Richard Rogers Partnership, London, England
CLIENT: Groupement Rhodanien de Construction
FUNCTION OF BUILDING: Shopping centre
LOCATION: Nantes, Brittany, France
SIZE: 21,000m²
DATE OF COMPLETION: 1987
ARCHITECTURAL INTENTION: The client, GRC, required a design for a building which could be used on two different sites and built in parallel. The building should have a strong identity with a long distance readability and respond to a very short construction period and a low budget. The brief was for a building with a gross area of 21,000m² spread over two floors, each with a floor to floor height of 6.5m. A two-storey building was designed, located in the middle of the site to the south of a small hill. The access to the main entrance is over a steel bridge which links the building with a public square. The building is serviced by road at the back and both sides. The main entrance to the building is at first floor level traversing through a large glass wall into a double height reception and entrance space with escalators serving both levels.

Sir Richard Rogers' Usine Centre near Nantes is part of an oeuvre by the same author who seeks to animate an otherwise dumb shed by placing the structural supporting systems on the outside of the enclosing fabric. The combination of colour and fine detailing raises the building beyond the mere utility of construction to a position of international architectural importance.

Nantes Shopping Centre continued over page

Nantes Shopping Centre continued

TRANSFERABLE LANGUAGE

Private houses, Delft

ARCHITECT: Cepezed B.V., Delft, Netherlands
CLIENT: Fam. Pesman and Fam. van Seyen
FUNCTION OF BUILDING: Private houses
LOCATION: Delft, Netherlands
SIZE: Site 600m^2; built area 168m^2
DATE OF COMPLETION: August 1990
ARCHITECTURAL INTENTION: This project presented a unique opportunity to put some architectural and technical experiments into practice. The house is designed as a single volume with one strong architectural element, three storeys high, which creates several levels and spaces.

At the front of the house, this element contains a service shaft. Behind this shaft, also within the element, the kitchen (ground floor), the bathrooms (2nd and 3rd level) and the service area are located. In the volume of the house(s) this service element is most significant in its architectural form. Two sliding-doors in the livingroom (4 meters high) open up the corner of the house to enjoy the scenery.

Apart from the foundations the groundfloor, and the party wall, the whole building is constructed from steel and glass. The sandwich panels, the elements of the kitchen, bathrooms and the perforated cladding on the service element are all made of stainless steel.

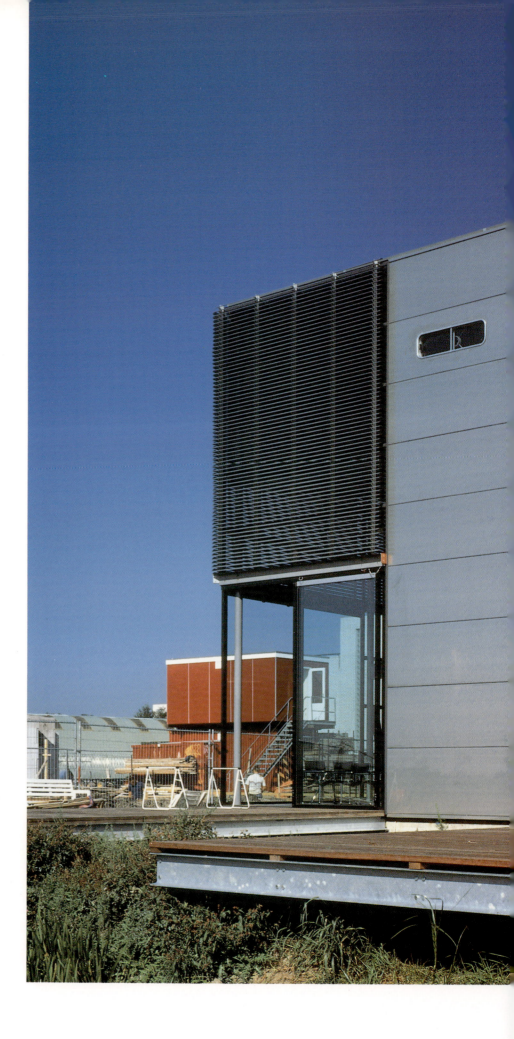

THE BEST IN INDUSTRIAL ARCHITECTURE

TRANSFERABLE LANGUAGE

Industrial Kitchen

ARCHITECT: Philippe Gazeau, Paris, France
CLIENT: Ville de Paris
FUNCTION OF BUILDING: Industrial kitchen
LOCATION: Paris, France
SIZE: 1,500m^2
DATE OF COMPLETION: September 1989
ARCHITECTURAL INTENTION: The main problem to solve with this industrial building was how to find ways to bring natural light into the heart of the work space and communication system (stairwells, passageways, corridors); the second problem was to successfully integrate the rather 'brutale' dimensions of a small factory with the lines of a Parisian street.

THE BEST IN INDUSTRIAL ARCHITECTURE

TRANSFERABLE LANGUAGE

Stansted Airport Terminal

ARCHITECT: Sir Norman Foster and Partners, London, England

CLIENT: BAA plc/Stansted Airport Limited

FUNCTION OF BUILDING: Airport terminal and ancillary buildings

LOCATION: Stansted Airport, Stansted, Essex, England

SIZE: 85,700m^2

DATE OF COMPLETION: March 1991

ARCHITECTURAL INTENTION: The configuration of the Stansted Airport Master Plan has orderly and clearly defined zones for its various activities. The terminal design responds to this by seeking the simplicity and convenience which characterized the earliest flying era. All public facilities are provided on a single concourse floor with arrivals and departures facilities planned side by side. The design gives a compact building which reduces walking distances for passengers and enables them to move through the building on simple linear routes. To allow the airport a high degree of flexibilty for future growth and modifications, all passenger facilities at concourse level which require enclosure, such as shops, banks, kitchens, left luggage, lavatories and medical facilities, have been designed as free-standing enclosures or cabins, which can be easily dismantled. These are 3.5 metres high and served by independent environmental engineering systems located in the undercroft.

Sir Norman Foster's terminal building for Stansted Airport in England is the apotheosis of the shed. A folded canopy is lowered to rest on a grid of structural trees to establish a kind of absolute architectonic shelter for the arrival and departure of planes, people and cargo.

Stansted Airport Terminal continued over page

THE BEST IN INDUSTRIAL ARCHITECTURE

Stansted Airport Terminal continued

TRANSFERABLE LANGUAGE

TRANSFERABLE LANGUAGE

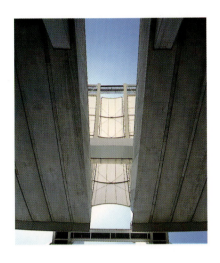

World Cup Football Stadium

ARCHITECT: Renzo Piano Building Workshop, Genoa, Italy

CLIENT: City of Bari, Italy

FUNCTION OF BUILDING: Football stadium (S. Nicola)

LOCATION: Bari, Italy

SIZE: 60,000 seats

DATE OF COMPLETION: 1990

ARCHITECTURAL INTENTION: Set amidst the Mediterranean nature of the region, the new Bari stadium raises from a deep crater rooted in the land of Puglia. It looks like a ring-shaped spaceship set all around a central stage, with a football pitch surrounded by an athletics track, sunken into the ground and surrounded by stands at ground level. It is only partially seen from the surrounding countryside as it is hidden by vegetation. The geometric design consists of a radial system of 26 axes to ensure greater safety and to ease the flow of people between the stadium and the parking area. The stadium is conceived to hold 60,000 people, all on individual seats, under the large teflon roofing, joined to the upper stands to which the lights are secured in a continuous line. The upper tribune is made of 312 precast crescent-shaped elements, assembled on site. Other functions, like toilets, box offices, bars, information desks and services are located on top of the hill under the 'portico' created by the upper stand. If there could be any such thing as a factory for collective euphoria then it must be the football stadium.

World Cup Football Stadium continued over page

World Cup Football Stadium continued

Studios and Galleries, Liverpool School of Architecture

ARCHITECT: Dave King and Rod McAllister, in association with the Herald Beech Partnership, Liverpool, England
CLIENT: University of Liverpool
FUNCTION OF BUILDING: New studio and galleries
LOCATION: Liverpool School of Architecture and Building Engineering, Liverpool, England
SIZE: 1,426m²
DATE OF COMPLETION: October 1988
ARCHITECTUREAL INTENTION: The New Studio and Galleries have been built as part of a scheme to extend the existing Liverpool School of Architecture building to accommodate the Department of Building Engineering. The design provides a completely open three-level atrium space interconnected by steel stairways and accessible from several different points within the existing school. The building projects a modern image within classical guidelines, using structural expression and display of services systems to help guide students in their understanding of building techniques. By this method, some of the mystery surrounding building technology is 'deconstructed' using a clear juxtaposition of elements in a logical framework, rather than a more fashionable jumble of elements. The exposure of jointing methods, rainwater disposal systems, heating and lighting sources for all to see is intended to be of educational benefit in that it allows students of architecture and building engineering to appreciate the complexity of environmental and structural and aesthetic forms using their own school environment as a model.

Natural Factories In his classic textbook, *Nature's Teachings*, J. Wentworth D'Arcy Thompson reviews the world of natural phenomena and offers a guide as to how plants, animals, birds and insects have made a fundamental contribution to the fields of art and science. Fritjof Capra's engaging thesis, *The Tao of Physics,* observes connections between post-Newtonian physics and early Chinese philosophy with similar references to the microscopic world of nature, while Edward de Zurko's *Origins of Functionalist Theory* reinforces the position observed by Ruskin and Morris, that function is *a priori* and innate in all matter. Conceptual thinking in the arts must therefore be physically and metaphysically referential to the world of natural things.

Frank Lloyd Wright, in his 'organic architecture', claimed an originality by calling for architects to eschew the academic tradition of Greco-Roman principles and return to what he described as 'the zero degree of architecture', namely an architecture inspired and driven by the natural phenomena that existed before the arguments and theories of Plato, Aristotle, Socrates and Pythagoras.

D'Arcy Thompson, de Zurko and Wright were all observing nature by way of recording the geometry and mathematics inherent in, say, the logarithmic spiral of fossilized crustacean and simply copying either the form type as the basis for an architectural plan, or applying the geometry as organizing system of proportion for the section of a great cathedral. However, there are lessons for architecture before the zero degree. The thesis is that Thompson el al are treating nature to a clinical audit, 'looking' at it with the eye of the scientist and discovering only the antecedents of tested or approved knowledge. In other words, they discover only what they expect to discover and what conforms to received ideas. Beyond the surfaces of things, there could be revealed a random, asymmetrical 'order' that could be extrapolated into a series of architectonic figures. Some experiments with photographic techniques – magnification, repeat imagery, photocopying processes – carried out on natural phenomena indicates that there may be another kind of order that does not conform to western rationalist precents but evokes an intuitive response. Such a response eludes description, simply because the vocabulary has not yet been compiled.

Although the natural factories – a quarry for making stone, or a windmill field for making electricity – are, to an extent, manmade, the quasi-architectural figure that has been established by the surreal juxtaposition of, for example thousands of tree-trunks floating on a pre-historical Canadian river or a forest of moving blades laid against a profane Californian landscape, is something which can be seen to contribute to the development of an architectural language before and beyond the modern world of critical thought.

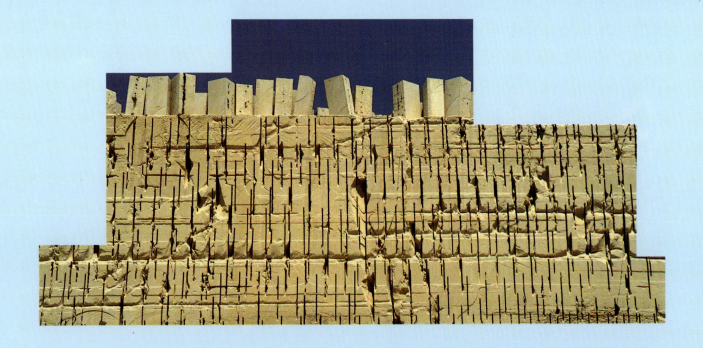

THE BEST IN INDUSTRIAL ARCHITECTURE

NATURAL FACTORIES

Mggarb Quarry No. 4, Gozo, Malta

THE BEST IN INDUSTRIAL ARCHITECTURE

Windfarm generating electric power, California, USA

NATURAL FACTORIES

Logdump, Queen Charlotte Island, British Columbia, Canada

Index of Projects

A

Advanced Textiles Products Factory, London, England 54–5
Asahi Brewery and Beer Hall, Tokyo, Japan 188–9

B

Becton Dickinson Labware Manufacturing Facility, Durham, North Carolina, USA 46–7
Blueprint Park, Southampton, Hampshire, England 137–9
Braun Factory and Headquarters, Melsungen, Germany 105–7

C

Canary Wharf Eastern Access Lifting Bridge and Control Building, London, England 48–9
Cargo Warehouse, Poyle, London, England 74–7
Centre d'Activités Zac de l'Ourcq, Paris, France 70–71
Cité Technique et Administrative, Paris, France 126–131
Clos Pegase Winery, Napa Valley, California, USA 182–6
Cummins Diesel Engine Factory, Shotts, Lanarkshire, Scotland 26–9

D

Dairy, Sem, Vestfold, Norway 178–9
Draught Beer Racking Plant, Bury St Edmunds, Suffolk, England 187

E

Exhaust Purification Plant, Oslo, Norway 156–7

F

The Factory, Manchester, England 36–9
Financial Times Building, London, England 56–61

G

Gateway One, Basingstoke, Hampshire, England 30–1
Grape Drying Towers, Turfan, China 190–1
Grianan Building, Dundee, Scotland 90–1

H

Historical Center of Industry and Labor, Youngstown, Ohio, USA 146–7
Hooke Park College, Dorset, England 120–3

I

Igualada Commercial Factory Warehouse, Barcelona, Spain 88–9
Incineration Plant, Budapest, Hungary 154–5
Industrial Kitchen, Paris, France 206–7
Inmos Microprocessor Factory, Newport, Gwent, Wales 96–103

K

Kensal Road Factories, London, England 80–5

L

Lambeth River Station, London, England 160–1

M

Majadahonda Water Purification Plant, Madrid, Spain 152–3
David Mellor Cutlery Factory, Hathersage, Derbyshire, England 34–5
Mggarb Quarry No. 4, Gozo, Malta 218–9

N

Nantes Centre Commercial, Nantes, France 200–3
Natural Gas Purification Plant, Emmen, Netherlands 144–5
Navy Weapons Workshop, Sydney, Australia 50–3

O

ORF Radio Station and Studios, Salzburg, Austria 40–1

P

P A Technology Center, Princeton, New Jersey, USA 14–5
Paper Warehouse, Belvedere, Kent, England 86–7
Power Station Offices, Tyssedal, Hardanger, Norway 166–7
Post Office, Budapest, Hungary 158–9
Private Houses, Delft, Netherlands 204–5

Processing Plant for the Budapest Pumphouse, Royal Victoria Dock, London, England 162–3

R

Recycling Plant for Domestic Waste, Oslo, Norway 140–2
Renault Distribution Centre, Swindon, Wiltshire, England 62–7

Research Laboratory for Experimental Traumatology, Ulm, Germany 116–7

S

SZLFI Laboratory, Szaszhalombatta, Hungary 118–9
J. Sainsbury Supermarket and Housing Development, London, England 194–9
Schlumberger Research Laboratory, Cambridge, England 108–11
Schwarzkopf Warehouse, Aylesbury, Buckinghamshire, England 72–3
Sewage Pumping Station, Reykjavik, Iceland 150–1
Simonds Farson Cisk Brewery, Mriehel, Malta 170–7
Speculative Factory Units, Waltham Cross, Hertfordshire, England 78–9
Speculative Light Industrial Units, Maidenhead, Berkshire, England 92–3
Stansted Airport Terminal, Stansted, Essex, England 208–11
Steelcase Industrial Center, Kentwood, Michigan, USA 32–3
Storm Water Pumping Station, London, England 148–9
Studio and Galleries, Liverpool School of Architecture, Liverpool, England 215

T

Tottenham Hale Station, London, England 143
Trebor Sweet Factory, Colchester, Essex, England 180–1

V

Vitra International Furniture Manufacturing Facility and Design Museum, Wiel-am-Rhein, Germany 42–5

W

WMI Environmental Monitoring Laboratory, Geneva, Illinois, USA 112–3
Water Control Towers, Estangeto, Pirineo de Lerida, Spain 132–3
Water Purification, Buitrago, Madrid, Spain 165
Water Purification Plant, Pinilla, Madrid, Spain 164
Water Treatment Centre, Reading, Berkshire, England 134–6
World Cup Football Stadium, Bari, Italy 212–4

Directory of Practising Designers

This directory lists the addresses of designers in current practice. While every effort has been made to ensure that this list was correct at the time of going to press, subsequent changes in address or status are beyond the publishers' remit.

A & D Studio
H–1122 Budapest
Varosmajor utca 74
Hungary
PROJECT: Incineration Plant 155–6

Iniki Abalos y Juan Herreros Arquitectos
Gran Via No 1–5 1
28013 Madrid
Spain
PROJECT: Majadahonda Water Purification Plant 153–4

Ahrends Burton & Koralek
Unit 1
7 Chalcot Road
London NW1 8LH
England
PROJECTS: Cummins Engine Co. Ltd 26–29; Hooke Park College 120–23

Alsop Lyall & Störmer
The Power House
Alpha Place
Flood Street
London SW3
England
PROJECT: Canary Wharf Eastern Access Lifting Bridge and Control Building 48–9; Lambeth River Station 161–2; Tottenham Hale Station 143

Arup Associates
37 Fitzroy Square
London W1P 6AA
England
PROJECT: Gateway One 30–1; Trebor Sweet Factory 180–1

Astrup og Hellern
Karoline Kristiansensvei 3
0661 Oslo
Norway
PROJECT: Recycling Plant for Domestic Waste 143–4

Broadway Malyan
3 Weybridge Business Park
Addlestone
Surrey KT15 2UN
England
PROJECT: Paper Warehouse 86

Cepezed
Phoenixstraat 58
Postbus 3068
2601 Delft
Netherlands
PROJECT: Private Houses at Delft 204–5

Paul Chemetov and Borja Huidobro
4 Square Massena
75013 Paris
France
PROJECT: Centre d'Activites Zac de l'Ourcq 70–1

Cristian Cirici & Associates
C/. Caspe 15
08013 Barcelona
Spain
PROJECT: Estangeto Water Control Towers 132–3

Conran Roche Architects
Nutmeg House
66 Gainsford Street
Butlers Whaft
London SE1 2NY
England
PROJECT: Mothercare Distribution Centre 87

Corea, Gallardo, Mannino Arquitectos Asociados
Copernico 43, 2° 3°
09821 Barcelona
Spain
PROJECT: Igualada Commercial Factory Warehouse 88–9

Denton Scott Architects
5 Mill Lane
Woolstones
Milton Keynes MK15 0AJ
England
PROJECT: Schwarzkopf Warehouse 72–3

Terry Farrell & Company
The Old Aero Works
17 Hatton Street
London NW8 8PL
England
PROJECT: Water Treatment Centre 134–6

Florance Eichbaum Esocoff King Architects
1100 New York Avenue NW
Washington DC 20005
USA
PROJECT: Becton Dickinson Labware Manufacturing Facility 46–7

Foster Associates
Riverside 3
Albert Wharf
22 Hester Road
London SW11 4AN
England
PROJECT: Renault Distribution Centre 63–7; Stansted Airport Terminal 208–12

4B Arkitekter A/S
Fredensborgveien 11
0177 Oslo
Norway
PROJECT: Exhaust Purification Plant 157–8

Alfredo Lozano Gardel Architect
Dr. Esquerdo, 91–2 D
28007 Madrid
Spain
PROJECT: Water Purification Plant, Pinilla 164; Water Purification Plant, Buitrago 165

Philippe Gazeau
17 rue Froment
75011 Paris
France
PROJECT: Industrial Kitchen 206–7

Frank O. Gehry & Associates Inc,
1520–B Cloverfield Boulevard
Santa Monica
California 90404
USA
PROJECT: Vitra International Furniture Manufacturing Facility and Design Museum 42–45

Michael Graves Architect
341 Nassau Street
Princeton
New Jersey 08540 USA
USA
PROJECTS: Clos Pegase Winery 182–6; Historical Center of Industry and Labor 147–8

Greiner Inc.
82 Ionia Avenue N.W.
Grand Rapids
Michigan 49503–3044
USA
PROJECT: Steelcase Industrial Center 32–3

Nicholas Grimshaw & Partners
1 Conway Street
Fitzroy Square
London W1P 5HA
England
PROJECTS: Financial Times Building 56–61; J. Sainsbury Supermarket and Housing Development 194–9

Hamminga & Haverkort
Angelsloerdijk 13b
Postbus 1160
7801 BD Emmen
Netherlands
PROJECT: Natural Gas Purification Plant 145–6

Michael Hopkins & Partners
27 Broadley Street
London NW1 6LG
England
PROJECTS: David Mellor Cutlery Factory 34–5; Draught Beer Racking Plant 187; Schlumberger Institute 108–10

Istvan Janaky
Iparterv
V. Türr Istvan u. 9
H 1052 Budapest
Hungary
PROJECT: SZFKI Laboratory 118–9

Jestico + Whiles Architects
14 Stephenson Way
London NW1 2HD
England
PROJECT: Speculative Factory Units 78–9

Michel Kagan Architect
36 Avenue Junot
75018 Paris
France
PROJECT: Cite Technique et Administrative 126–131

Ben Kelly Design
10 Stoney Street
London SE1 9AD
England
PROJECT: The Factory 36–9

King McAllister
58 Park Lane
Liverpool L17 8UU
England
PROJECT: Studio and Galleries, Liverpool School of Architecture 215

Kisho Kurokawa Architect
Aoyama Building
2–3 Kita-aoyama 1–chome
Minato-ku
Tokyo
Japan
PROJECT: Nittokuno Research Center 111

LBR
Hamang Terrasa 55
Postboks 248
N–1301 Sandvika
Norway
PROJECT: Dairy 178–9

Nicholas Lacey Jobst & Partners
Reeds Wharf
33 Mill Street
London SE1 2BA
England
PROJECT: Advanced Textile Products Factory 54–5

LOG ID
Sindelfinger Strasse 85
Glashaus
7400 Tübingen
Germany
PROJECT: Research Laboratory for Experimental Traumatology 116–7

Nicoll Russell
Westfield Road
Broughton Fields
Dundee DD5 1ED
Scotland
PROJECT: The Grianan Building 90–91

John Outram Partnership
16 Devonshire Place
London W1N 1PB
England
PROJECTS: Cargo Warehouse at Poyle 74–7; Kensal Road Factories 80–5; Storm Water Pumping Station 149–50

Gustav Peichl
Opernring 4
A 1010 Vienna
Austria
PROJECT: ORF Radio Station and Studios

Perkins & Will
123 North Wacker Drive
Chicago
Illinois 60606
USA
PROJECT: WMI Environmental Monitoring Laboratory 112–3

Renzo Piano Building Workshop Srl
Piazza San Mateo 15
Philippe Starck Product
3 rue de la Roquette
75011 Paris
France
PROJECT: Asahi Brewery and Beer Hall 188–9

James Stirling, Michael Wilford and Associates
8 Fitzroy Square
London W1PH 5AH
England
PROJECT: Braun Factory and Headquarters 104–7

Thorpe Architecture
Sparks Yard
Tarrant Street
Arundel
West Sussex BN18 9SB
England
PROJECT: Blueprint Park 137–9

Photographic Acknowledgements

AA = Architectural Association

p 6 **Roger Viollett**; p 7 **Mansell Collection**; p 8 **Bulloz**; p 9 **Bulloz**; p 10 **Roger Viollett**; p 11T **Foto Marburg**; p 11B **Ullstein Bilderdienst**; p 12T **Foto Marburg**; p 12B **Foto Marburg**; p 13T **Foto Marburg**; p 13b **Ullstein Bilderdienst**; p 14 **RIBA Library**; p 16/17 **RIBA Library**; p 19 **RIBA Library**; p 20 **Marc Lieberman/Salk Institute**; p 21 **Jim Cox/Salk Institute**; p 22/3 **Ahrends Burton Koralek**; p 26–9 **Ahrends Burton Koralek**; p 28 **John Donat/Ahrends, Burton Koralek**; p 30/1 **Tony Weller/AA**; p 32/33 **Glen Calvin Moon/Davernam Associates**; p 34T **Michael Hopkins & Partners**; p 34BL **Richard Waite/Arcaid**; p 34BR **Richard Waite/Arcaid**; p 35 **Alberto Piovann/Arcaid**; p 36/7/8/9 **Julie Phipps/Arcaid**; p 40/41 **Hazel Coot/AA**; p 42/3/4/5 **Richard Bryant/Arcaid**; p 46/7 **Roger Ball Photography**; p 48/9 **Alsop Lyall and Störmer**; p 50/1/2/3 **Max Dupain**; p 54/5 **Martin Charles**; p 56/7/8/9 **Jo Reid and John Peck**; p 60 **Richard Bryant/Arcaid**; p 61 **Jo Reid and John Peck**; p 62–7 **Richard Bryant/Arcaid**; p 70/1 **M. Robinson**; p 71TL **J. M. Monthiers**; p 72/3 **Peter Cook/Denton Scott**; p 74/5/6/7 **John Outram Partnership**; p 78/9 **Jo Reid and John Peck**; p 80 **John Outram Partnership**; p 81T **Jo Reid and John Peck**; p 81B **John Outram Partnership**; p 82/3/4/5 **John Outram Partnership**; p 86 **Ian Knaggs**; p 87 **Conran Roches**; p 88/9 **Correa Gallardo Mannino Arquitectos**; p 90/1 **Alastair Hunter**; p 92/3 **Richard Bryant/Arcaid**; p 96/7 **Ken Kirkwood**; p 98/9 **Richard Bryant/Arcaid**; p 100/1 **Richard Bryant/Arcaid**; p 102/3 **Ken Kirkwood**; p 104/5/6/7 **Richard Bryant/Arcaid**; p 108T **Ove Arup**; p 108B **Valerie Bennett/AA**; p 109 **Mark Feinnes/Arcaid**; p 110 **Michael Hopkins and Partners**; p 111 **Tomio Ohashi**; p 112 **George Lambros/Perkins & Will**; p 114/5 **Otto Baitz/Richard Rogers Partnership**; p 116/7 **R. Blunck/LOG ID**; p 118/9 **Zoltán Szathmáry**; p 120/1/2/3 **Peter Cook/Ahrends Burton Koralek**; p 126/7/8/9 **J. M. Monthiers**; p 130/1 **J. M. Monthiers**; p 132/3 **Lluis Casals**; p 134/5/6/7 **Richard Bryant/Arcaid**; p 138/9 **Thorpe Architects**; p 138B **Matthew Weinreb**; p 140/1/2 **Kvaerner Brug/Astrup og Hellern**; p 143 **Alsop, Lyall and Störmer**; p 144/5 **PRP/British Steel**; p 146/7 **William Taylor/Michael Graves Architects**; p 148/9 **John Outram Partnership**; p 150/1 **Björn Hallson**; p 152/3 **Antxon Hernandez**; p 154/5 **Tibor Zsitva**; p 157/7 **Tiegens Fotoatelier**; p 158/9 **Zoltán Szathmáry**; p 160/1 **Alsop, Lyall and Störmer**; p 162/3 **Halcrow/Richard Rogers Partnership**; p 164/5 **Alfredo Lozano Gardel**; p 166/7 **Bjarne Eidnes A/S**; p 170/2/4/5/6/7 **Peter Cook**; p 178/9 **Olav Dahl/Tiegens Fotoatelier**; p 180/1 **Martin Charles/Ove Arup**; p 182/3/4/5/6 **Paschall/Taylor/Michael Graves Architect**; p 187 **Michael Hopkins and Partners**; p 188/9 **Koji Murakoshi/AA**; p 190/1 **François Ward/AA**; p 195/6/7/8/9 **Richard Bryant/Arcaid**; p 200/1/2/3 **Richard Bryant/Arcaid**; p 204/5 **PRP/British Steel**; p 206/7 **J. M. Monthiers/Phillipe Gazeau**; p 208/9 **Richard Bryant/Arcaid**; p 210/211 **Richard Bryant/Arcaid**; p 212/13/14 **Peter Cook/Arcaid**; p 215 **PRP/British Steel**; p 218/9 **Michael Potter/AA**; p 220 **Osman Vlora/AA**; p 221 **Canadian High Commission**.